Two-Dimensional Man

An essay on the
anthropology of
power and symbolism
in complex society

Abner Cohen

University of California Press

Berkeley and Los Angeles

University of California Press
Berkeley and Los Angeles, California
© Abner Cohen 1974
First Paperback Edition, 1976
ISBN: 0-520-03241-1
Library of Congress Catalog Card Number: 72-93525
Printed in the United States of America

1 2 3 4 5 6 7 8 9 0

For Sara

Contents

CONTENTS

Foreword to
the paperback edition

Since the publication of this book, about two years ago, there has been growing evidence that social anthropology is moving to a new ethnographic and theoretical phase, in which great attention is given to the study of complex society. Nowhere is this development so dramatic as in the USA, where increasing numbers of students and professional anthropologists are turning to the study of the dynamic socio-cultural processes and complexities of American cities.

Two main features that characterise these cities are central to the anthropological enterprise. One is the *cultural heterogeneity* of their populations: the immense variety of their symbolic forms, styles of life, networks of primary relationships, and religious, ethnic, and racial ideologies. The other is the *intense struggle for power*, both economic and political, among varieties of groupings within the same populations: power elites, political parties, business and professional organisations, labour unions, crowds, radicals, criminal gangs, youth movements, and all sorts of other associations. The analysis of the sociological relations, of the causal interconnections, between these two features, as they manifest themselves in the behaviour and biographies of men, is the particular domain of social anthropology. The main endeavour of this book is to suggest how such analysis may be undertaken. The last three chapters can be particularly helpful to students.

The focus is on the structure of informally organised power groups—which tend to articulate their organisation in terms of cultural strategies—their rise and fall, and the processes of change in their symbolic forms in response to changes in the wider power systems within which they are encapsulated. The city's large population makes possible the formation of diverse groupings of this type, its density makes the interaction between them intense, and its anonymity enhances their tendency to be exclusive and 'invisible'.

This concentration on the study of socio-cultural groupings is a *heuristic* measure, devised to enable the anthropologist to apply his micro-sociological techniques to the study of the complexity of the massive city. It need not entail a subscription to pluralism as a political ideology, nor lead—as some Marxists fear—to the reification of groups and, consequently, to the legitimation of the capitalist system of which they are a part. It is no substitute for the study of the 'total structure' of capitalism or of the state. But it can contribute substantially to the analysis of that structure because it deals with a dimension of power which has so far been little explored by students of industrial society. 'Classes' and 'power elites' cannot be comprehended without the analysis of the symbolic mechanisms (such as descent, patterns of socialisation, styles of life) that knit their members and families together and transform them from mere categories of people to concrete, cohesive, cooperating, and relatively enduring groupings. Marx saw classes as groups in this sense.

The significance of this dimension of power can be seen clearly in C. Wright Mills' study of *The Power Elite*. Mills' central argument is that the apparently separate, dispersed, and autonomous economic, political and military elites in the USA are in fact informally linked together into one powerful 'ruling elite' by the symbolic mechanisms of their style of life. Yet Mills devotes to this crucial part of his analysis only a few pages, not only because he lacks the necessary information, but also because the study of cultural symbols, and of their dynamic involvement in the relations of power, requires special concepts and techniques of investigation, under a different academic tradition. And it is this gap in the study of industrial society that social anthropology can fill.

Thus, the analysis of the dynamics of culture and power in the cities will shed substantial light on the study of the structure of power within much wider systems and will provide a unique contribution to the social sciences in general.

ABNER COHEN
London, May 1976

Preface

This book explores the possibilities of a systematic study of the dynamic interdependence between power relationships and symbolic action in complex society. A good deal of analysis in this field has been carried out by social anthropologists in the course of studying small-scale, simple, pre-industrial societies. The book will therefore examine the extent to which the theories, concepts, methods and techniques of social anthropology can be adapted for the study of modern complex societies in both developing and developed countries.

In both simple and industrial societies there are extensive patterns of normative, non-rational, non-utilitarian behaviour which play crucial parts in the distribution, maintenance and exercise of power. Descriptively, these are usually referred to as customs or, simply, as culture. On a higher level of analysis and abstraction they can be described as symbols.

Symbols are objects, acts, concepts, or linguistic formations that stand *ambiguously* for a multiplicity of disparate meanings, evoke sentiments and emotions, and impel men to action. They usually occur in stylised patterns of activities like ceremonial, ritual, gift exchange, prescribed forms of joking, taking an oath, eating and drinking together.

Many writers refer to all or some of the types of phenomena that are here described as symbols by using different terms, like 'culture', 'custom', 'norms', 'values', 'myths', 'rituals'. The term 'culture' is extensively used in many different senses and is too wide in its different connotations to be useful in operational microsociological studies. Both 'culture' and 'custom' cover also patterns of action that are utilitarian and technical and are subsumed under what I call 'the power order'. The terms 'norms' and 'values' are highly abstract and tend to connote meanings that are vague, subjective, and individual. The term 'myth' has been used by writers like Cassirer (1946) and MacIver (1947) in a wide enough sense to give some of the meanings covered by the term 'symbol'. Thus MacIver (*ibid.*, 4–5) writes:

> Every society is held together by a myth-system. . . . All social relations, the very texture of human society, are myth-born and myth-sustained. . . . Wherever he goes, whatever he encounters, man spins about him his web of myth, as the caterpillar spins its cocoon. Every individual spins his own variant within the greater web of the whole group.

Although MacIver contrasts 'myth' with 'technique' he subsumes under it what we nowadays call 'thought categories'. This usage of the term 'myth' is too general, imprecise, subjective and individual to be of much use in analysis, and is above all at variance with the more usual sense of 'fictitious narrative', in which it is used by most anthropologists. The term 'ritual' has similarly been used in an extensive sense to cover a wide range of patterns of normative action. Among social anthropologists this usage has been particularly developed by Leach (1954), with whose position I am in full agreement. Unfortunately, the majority of scholars have been using the term in a more technical sense, restricting it to only those ceremonial activities that have reference to 'mystical beings', or to 'the sacred'. The term 'symbol' overcomes many of the difficulties posed by these different terms, as it refers to phenomena that are objective and collective and are thus observable and verifiable, and it covers a wide range of cultural phenomena, though it is precise enough to indicate normative patterns of action, in contrast with utilitarian and technical patterns.

For the individual, symbols are fundamental mechanisms for the development of selfhood and for tackling the perennial problems of human existence, like life and death, good and evil, misery and happiness, fortune and misfortune. Although they can be said to be phenomena *sui generis*, existing in their own right and observed for their own intrinsic values, they are nearly always manipulated, consciously or unconsciously, in the struggle for, and maintenance of, power between individuals and groups. They may be said to be 'expressive'; but they are at the same time instrumental. The ceremonials of authority do not just reflect authority but create and recreate it. Political Man is also Symbolist Man. Man is two-dimensional.

The discussion focuses on the processes whereby interest groups manipulate different types of symbolic formations and symbolic patterns of action to articulate a number of basic organisational functions, like distinctiveness and communication. A group is formally organised when its aims are specified and its organisation is rationally planned on bureaucratic lines. As Weber shows, this kind of organisation is the most effective type of human organisation. But even in the advanced liberal industrial societies there are structural conditions under which some interest groups cannot organise themselves on formal lines. Resort is therefore made to articulate the organisation of the group on informal bases, making use of kinship, friendship, ritual, ceremonial and other forms of symbols and of symbolic activities that are implicit in what is known as 'style of life'. The difference between formal and informal group organisation is a matter of degree and nearly all groups fall on one continuum from the most formally organised to the most informally organised. The organisation of an interest group can thus be conceived as having two dimensions, the contractual and the normative, or the formal and the informal.

Throughout this book, 'power' is taken to be an aspect of nearly all social relationships, and 'politics' to be referring to the processes involved in the distribution, maintenance, exercise and struggle for power. Some political scientists object to this 'extensive' definition principally on the ground that it makes the study of politics co-extensive with the study of all society. But this objection is mainly methodological and not theoretical. Most political scientists are fully aware of the fact that power does not exist in a 'pure form' but is always inherent in social relationships of varying types. There is no short cut to solving the problem, and techniques must be found to study power in its various manifestations. This is a central issue which is discussed in detail in many parts of the essay.

PREFACE

I have tried to present the discussion as simply as possible. This is not only because the book is addressed to students of the behavioural sciences generally, some of whom may not be familiar with social anthropological jargon. But also because I firmly believe that we can advance our disciplines greatly by 'demystifying' our formulations. Indeed, one of the crucial tests of the validity and significance of a sociological observation is to try to express it in simple language. It is surprising how many of our pet 'theories' fail in this test and turn out to be but banal tautologies.

I am grateful to Professor Ernest Gellner for commenting on an earlier draft of a part of this book and to the editor of *Man*, the journal of the Royal Anthropological Institute, for permitting me to reproduce parts of my paper: 'Political anthropology: the analysis of the symbolism of power relations' (*Man*, 4, 1969:215–35). My thanks are also due to my many students in the UK and, occasionally, in the USA for their untiring polemic about many of the theoretical issues that are raised here.

ABNER COHEN

Introduction: the bizarre and the mystical in modern society

The hidden dimension of organisation
Psychological and culturological explanations
Orientations in sociology and political science
The approach from political anthropology
Outline of the argument

The hidden dimension of organisation

The view, implicit in the evolutionary formulations of Weber and others, that modern society is distinct from primitive society in being organised on the basis of contract, in being secular, rational, manipulative and impersonal, has recently been seriously challenged by many students of society. A rapidly accumulating body of evidence indicates that the bizarre and the exotic in the patterns of social behaviour are not the exclusive monopoly of pre-industrial societies. In many situations in modern society custom is as strange and as sovereign as it is in 'primitive' society.

Scholars are now 'rediscovering' in modern society the existence and significance of an endless array of patterns of symbolic behaviour that have been for long associated exclusively with 'primitive' society.

1

In the field of interpersonal relationships, numerous studies have been carried out of extended kinship relations, different types of friendship, ritualised relationships, and a host of other types of 'informal', non-contractual, relationships that pervade the whole fabric of social life. Extensive studies in the USA and UK show that a great deal of business is arranged and regulated, not by the law of contract, but by non-contractual mechanisms. Studies of the City of London have indicated that millions of pounds worth of transactions are concluded daily without the use of documents, through the mechanisms of customary rules and practices that are observed within a distinct culture group—the City men.

In the field of ritual, the revival of religious activities among a large proportion of the population of the USA has been reported by scholars. In the UK, although Sunday attendance in church has dwindled, the demand on organised religion for rites of passage continues with little change (Wilson 1969:22). About four million Americans and three-quarters of a million Britons are affiliated within what has been described as the greatest secret society on earth—Freemasonry (Dewar 1966). The overwhelming majority of these men are from the wealthy and professional classes. They meet periodically in their local centres and, behind the locked and well-guarded doors of their temples, they wear the colourful and elaborately embroidered regalia, carry the jewels, swords and other emblems of office, and perform their 'ancient' rituals. These rituals, and the beliefs that are associated with them, are as dramatic and as strange as those found in any tribal society in Africa. The 'rediscovery of the supernatural' has been discussed by many writers (see, for example, Berger 1969) and surveys of superstitious beliefs and practices in modern society have been made by others (see Jahoda 1969), indicating massive preoccupation with such esoteric activities as fortune telling, witchcraft and sorcery. In a recent official document, Sir John Foster reports that a large number of persons in Britain today are members of 'Scientology', a pseudo-religious, pseudo-scientific organisation (Foster 1971). One may also mention here the many types of 'hippy' groupings that have been formed during the last decade, with their own brands of ecstatic and mystical pursuits. Youths from Europe and the USA halt their university studies to trek reverently to the mystics of the Orient hoping to find new formulae for explaining the meaning of life in modern society.

In numerous cases, ritual behaviour merges indistinguishably with so-called ceremonial behaviour. In every hour of the day, public dramas are enacted by the state, by groups of all sorts, and by persons interacting with other persons. One may include under this heading such patterns of symbolic behaviour as those manifested in manners, etiquette, dress, gift and visit exchanges, eating and drinking together. As Goffman (1969) shows, all our behaviour is in fact couched in endless series of dramatic performances.

Another type of symbolic behaviour can be found in the organisation of play of all sorts, sports and leisure-time activities. Yet another important related field of activity is that of popular art and drama that is daily presented to millions of people in cinemas, radio and television programmes, newspapers, books and on the stage.

All this is true, not only of capitalist societies, as Marx maintained, but also of socialist societies that are officially organised under 'scientific communism'. Here emblems, slogans, banners, mass parades, titles, patriotic music and songs and, inevitably, the 'world view' of dialectical materialism—these and a host of all sorts of other symbolic forms play their part in the maintenance of the political order. The cost in time, effort and resources, for both individuals and groups in staging and performing these symbolic activities is colossal.

Psychological and culturological explanations

Some of these patterns of symbolic action have sometimes been explained, or rather explained away, historically, as 'cultural lags'. However, although many of them are indeed survivals from the past, they continue into the present, not because of inertia or of conservatism, but because they play important roles within the contemporary social settings. Indeed some of them are revived from the past to serve in the same way. Others are of recent origin and yet others are being continuously created for new, or for old, purposes. The history of a cultural trait will tell us very little about its social significance within the situation in which it is found at present. Thus as I show later (pp. 91-8), although ethnicity involves the extensive use of old customs and traditions, it is not itself the outcome of cultural conservatism or continuity. The continuities of customs are certainly there, but their functions have changed.

3

Within the contemporary situation ethnicity is essentially a political phenomenon, as traditional customs are used only as idioms and as mechanisms for political alignments.

Similarly, although symbolic action is always involved in psychic processes, psychology cannot by itself explain the nature of these symbolic forms. Collective ritual is not the product of recurring spontaneous individual creativity resulting from recurring psychic states. On the contrary, for the majority of people it is the ritual that recreates certain psychic states in the minds of the participants, not the other way round. The ritual might have been originally the spontaneous creation of an individual with exclusive autonomous subjective experience, like a prophet or an artist. But once the created symbols are adopted by a group, they are no longer subjective or individual. They become objective, in the sense that they confront the members of the group as things that exist outside their psyches and that will constrain them in their behaviour. They also become public, the collective representations of a group.

As I show later, psychology can certainly shed light on the nature of the psychic 'origin' of symbolic action in general. It can contribute significantly towards the analysis of symbolic and artistic creativity and of the psychic experience which is induced by the performance of ceremonials and rituals. But the social significance of symbolic action can be discovered only when it is studied within the context of social relationships. Symbolic action is an essential process for the development of selfhood, but its patterns are provided by society and are always loaded with social consequences, many of which are unintended by the actors. Thus the same pattern of symbolic action has both psychological and social consequences at one and the same time. To put it differently, the same phenomenon, namely symbolic action, can be explained psychologically and sociologically. But these explanations are different and are developed within two separate conceptual schemes. Even if they may sometimes support one another or shed light on one another, they should nevertheless be kept analytically separate and not confused one with the other (see Leach 1958; Gluckman 1964, 1968; Turner 1964).

Some serious attempts have been made to explain symbolic forms in their own right, in terms of their own 'logic'. Two major orientations can be mentioned here. The one of a number of individual scholars who envisage the development of a 'science of symbolic behaviour'. Some interesting, intelligent and imaginative formulations in the 'interpretation' of symbolic forms have been made by these scholars. But these formulations have often been conjectural, non-verifiable, non-cumulative, 'meanings' attributed to symbols and are mostly arrived at by sheer intuition and individual guess-work. The studies by these writers have inevitably been 'undisciplined', in the sense that they have had no specific aim or frame of reference and have often wandered in different directions, mixing metaphysics with logic, art, psychology, theology, linguistics and history, frequently marshalling impressive arrays of inspiring statements, intuitions, apt illustrations and quotations. Above all, they offer no clear programme for further research and no indication how the subject is to be developed. I believe that this is why writers like Langer (1964) and Geertz (1964), who hoped to develop such a science, complain of how little has been achieved.

The other orientation is the more systematic attempt by Lévi-Strauss and by the proliferating 'schools' of his followers, to explain symbolic behaviour in terms of a logical structure underlying all human thinking. But, as I indicate later, this is made at the expense of ignoring the social actor – political man – with the result that the analysis fails to deal with the dynamics of interaction between men in society. Symbols in Lévi-Strauss's system are logical categories, while in the dynamics of socio-cultural life they are 'valences', being not only cognitive, but also agitative and conative.

Orientations in sociology and political science

Symbolic action can be systematically analysed only when it is related to other variables with which it is significantly inter-connected. Public, or collective, symbols are essentially objective and are intimately related to social factors. Some important contributions to their analysis have been made within sociology. As Parsons (1951:1-16) puts it, 'the central concern of sociological theory is with the phenomena of institutionalisation'. 'Institutionalisation' writes Blau (1969:67, 71) 'refers to the processes that perpetuate a social pattern and make it endure . . . and thus outlast the lives of human beings.' Underlying the whole phenomenon of institutionalisation is the symbolisation process. Social relations are developed and maintained through symbolic forms and action. The great sociologists, among them Marx, Weber, Durkheim, Edmund Burke, greatly illuminated the sociological interconnections between

5

social relations and symbolic action. More recently, some important contributions in this respect have been made by sociologists in the study of norms and values, in the development of the sociology of religion, of art, and of thought systems. But a number of factors – practical, theoretical, methodological and epistemological – have seriously thwarted the development of a sociology of symbolic behaviour (for a discussion of some of these problems see Duncan 1968 and 1969).

Sociology has been developed in the study of the advanced socially differentiated industrial societies of the West. These are highly complex societies with a bewildering array of formal and of less formal groupings, representing a variety of interests, competing, federating and manoeuvring to achieve their ends. Often increasing *differentiation* and *specialisation* result in the separation between a group and its legitimating cult of symbolic formations. In this way ideologies become separately organised and the links between them and the groups that created them become blurred or 'hidden'. In due course the now autonomous symbolic cult is adopted by other interest groups and its function may thereby be drastically changed. More frequently, the same cult can serve different interest groups, providing each with different organisational functions. Further differentiation leads to the fragmentation of the cult into specialised sectors, each promoted by a separate organisation. An interest group may thus construct its cult from drawing on the formulations and services of different cult organisations like churches. For example, in their efforts to articulate an informal organisation to co-ordinate their political activities, the Creoles of Sierra Leone have adopted a variety of beliefs and practices from organised church religion, from the Freemasonic order, and from other specialised organisations (for details see below pp. 83-4, 107-9, 112-18).

The complexity resulting from all this is further intensified through the dynamics of *change* which affect the different elements of a group organisation differently, so that some elements will change, while others will hardly change, though their functions may alter. And, as these societies are large in scale, a holistic view of symbolic forms and social relationships will be almost impossible.

At the same time, sociologists have inevitably been forced to specialise, some in different types of social relations, others – few in number – in symbolic systems. And as sociologists have often been keen to develop their research on 'scientific lines', they tended to apply rigorous quantification to the phenomena they studied. Gradually this has led to a concentration on easily quantifiable phenomena and to the neglect of phenomena that are not given to intensive quantitive analysis.

As symbolic formations and action are essentially dramatistic and are thus not given to direct and precise measurement, less and less sociologists have bothered to study them. Imperceptibly, the phenomena that are not studied come to be regarded as sociologically insignificant and this perpetuates further the view that modern society is predominantly secular, manipulative and rational. But how will the process of institutionalisation, which is regarded as the central concern of sociological theory, be analysed without the detailed analysis of symbolic forms and action?

Political science solves the problems of institutional differentiation and of scale by concentrating on the study of one variable-power, within the total universe of the state. Instead of studying the vaguely conceived 'social relationships' with which sociology is concerned, it concentrates on the study of power relationships, of subordination, superordination, and equality in various combinations. But of course this solution is accomplished by political science at the expense of its becoming an essentially descriptive endeavour. In the words of one of its practitioners (Young 1968:5), its effort is mainly 'to delineate relevant phenomena, to generate useful classifications and breakdowns, and to pinpoint the important characteristics of political activities'. Furthermore, even the descriptive picture tends in the work of many political scientists to be limited to the organisation and activities of the state and of formally organised groupings within the state.

Some political scientists extend the domain of their study to include the political aspects of formally non-political institutions, such as religion, and thereby come closer to the study of the relation between symbolic action and power relations. Some of them have been concerned with the study of 'influence', usually that of business, within local communities. Others have studied political, mainly state, symbols. But these studies have been marginal and the scholars engaged in them are often branded as 'political sociologists'. Their research has been fragmentary, without forming a special 'school' through the accumulation of their findings. Their analysis has not been systematic. Above all, they suffer from an implicit assumption that political symbols are consciously intended symbols

7

and when some of them write of 'political socialisation' their accounts are mechanical and unidimensional. And this leads the discussion to another major difficulty in the study of symbolism in modern society.

Most of sociology and political science have been developed by scholars studying their own societies. This means that these scholars are themselves personally caught up in the same body of symbols which they try to decode. Most symbols are largely rooted in the unconscious mind and are thus difficult to identify and analyse by people who live under them. As the proverb says: It is hardly a fish that can discover the existence of water. The very concepts and categories of thought which sociologists and political scientists employ in their analysis are themselves part of the very political ideology which they try to understand. It is true that this paradox (Mannheim 1936) can to some extent be resolved by the slow, cumulative, empirical and comparative research. But little has been achieved in this way so far. This is not only because sociologists and political scientists are directed in the choice of problems for research by the donors of research funds (usually interest groups, including the state) and by the current problems of the day. But because there is an element of nihilism in this line of research. Symbols are essential for the development and maintenance of social order. To do their job efficiently their social functions must remain largely unconscious and unintended by the actors. Once these functions become known to the actors, the symbols lose a great deal of their efficacy. This is one of the reasons why students of society are often so 'revolutionary'. But against this, it can be argued that the symbols of society are manipulated by interest groups for their own benefits and that unless we understand the nature of the symbols and of the ways in which they are manipulated we shall be exploited without our knowledge. This of course is a meta-sociological issue, concerning the uses of sociology. But the paradox that Mannheim posed is there and it is a problem that is at the basis of all social science, more particularly so at the basis of any politico-symbolic analysis.

The approach from political anthropology

The methodological problems of differentiation, scale and the paradox of sociological knowledge that have impeded the develop-

ment of a sociology of symbolic behaviour, have been easily overcome by social anthropologists in the course of their studies in pre-
industrial societies. These societies have had relatively simple
technologies, little institutional differentiation, and have been
small in scale. The anthropologist working on them has very often
been a stranger from a different culture, and was thus in a better
position than either the native or the sociologist studying his own
society to study the social significance of symbolic behaviour.

I must hasten to say that even under these methodologically and
epistemologically favourable conditions, social anthropology has
not yet developed into a well-defined discipline. Some of what goes
on under its banner is descriptive ethnography with little original
analysis or theory. Sociologists are sometimes right in saying that
what saves some anthropologists is their ethnography. Readers of
anthropological monographs usually find intrinsic interest in the
accounts of the strange customs of other peoples, even when they
find little or no theory in these monographs. If you take away
ethnography from some anthropological monographs there will be
very little left which is of sociological significance. This is only partly
due to the emphasis placed by anthropologists on empirical field
data and to their initial reservations against speculative armchair
theorising. Social anthropology began by criticising sociology for
having a methodology but no subject-matter; it has itself so far
ended by having a great deal of subject-matter but relatively little
methodology or theory. Indeed a few leading social anthropologists
have expressed serious doubts about the possibility of developing a
science of society, and Evans-Pritchard (1963) has gone so far as to
state that a whole century of extensive studies in comparative
sociology and anthropology has yielded not a single formulation
similar to those discovered by the natural sciences. And, in his
recent Frazer Lecture, George Murdock (1972) described all
theorising in anthropology as being mythological, philosophical or
theological, and concluded that anthropology's only contribution
to knowledge is its colossal ethnography.

These extreme views however are concerned principally with problems facing all the social sciences and not anthropology alone. Despite its many shortcomings, social anthropology has made important
achievements in the sociological analysis of symbolism. Considering
the small number of its practitioners and the very limited resources
that have been allocated to its development, it has been unique in the

9

whole history of socio-cultural studies in that it has produced a cumulative body of hypotheses about the social significance of the symbolism of kinship, ritual and ceremonial. It can thus shed substantial light on the nature and processes of institutionalisation within a wide comparative perspective. What is more, anthropologists are no longer confining themselves to the study of tribal societies. Their research now extends to cover peasant societies under the great literate traditions of Islam, Hinduism, Buddhism and Christianity. There is already a great deal of anthropological literature on communities in India, Burma, the Middle East, North Africa and Latin America. In Africa and elsewhere research is no longer confined to rural areas but is being carried out also in urban centres to deal with more intensive and complex areas of social life where the struggle for economic and political power within the framework of modern state organisations is intense. As Firth points out (1951:18), although its techniques are 'micro-sociological', its formulations can be 'macro-sociological'.

But the question should still be explored whether social anthropology can adapt itself to the study of modern, large-scale complex societies *without losing its identity*, i.e. without thereby becoming sociology, political science or economics.

Social anthropologists are themselves being forced by a variety of circumstances into facing this question. The 'primitive' societies in whose study they have specialised are being rapidly incorporated within the new developing states whose formal structure is similar to that of the more developed countries. The need to analyse the processes underlying socio-cultural change in both the developing and the developed societies has become crucial.

It is symptomatic of all this that students of anthropology are no longer intellectually stimulated by ethnographic subject-matter alone. Many of them now come to the university after having been exposed to foreign cultures, and the accounts of the bizarre customs of traditional tribal societies no longer excite their imagination. In the age of the jumbo jet, of international youth organisations, of schemes for the exchange of students between countries, and of mass media of information and communication, ethnography is no longer news. The lesson of cultural relativism, that our culture is not the only valid one, has already sunk in. Indeed some of our youth continue to be concerned with exotic cultures but, paradoxically enough, they do so in an attempt, not to learn about the customs of those cultures, but to gain insights into the meaning of the life of man in contemporary society, the rational and the non-rational in his behaviour, his creativity and destructiveness, his potentialities and his ultimate destiny.

Equally symptomatic, though for different reasons, are the increasing difficulties which anthropologists encounter now in getting access to their 'traditional subject-matter'. The new states of the Third World have accumulated a strong dislike of anthropologists whom they often associate with reaction and imperialism. Although many of these states can and do benefit a great deal from the work of anthropologists, they are more interested in the study of the problems of the day: economic development, political modernisation, urbanisation, migration and employment. It has recently become difficult – in some cases indeed impossible – for anthropologists to get entrance permits to many of the developing countries. Even when an anthropologist is 'fostered' by a university department in the country where he wants to do research, he has to wait for several months to get an entry permit. Although this seems to be an unreasonable policy on the part of those governments, it can easily be seen as an index to a fundamental bias in anthropology, resulting from the experience of the colonial period. Until very recently, the anthropologist has usually been a citizen of the colonial power while those studied by him have been natives of colonies or of former colonies. This has been imperceptibly built into the very methodology and concepts of field work and of analysis. Even when a few anthropologists carried out their studies within developed countries, or within their own countries, they were led by a number of factors to study groupings that are regarded as low in social status, like farming settlements, working-class urban centres and immigrants from underdeveloped countries. The same tendency has been observed within sociology itself. Sociological 'field work' has very often been carried out by sociologists from a middle-class social background among working-class populations.

More significant than these 'exterior' factors is the theoretical and methodological cross-roads at which social anthropology finds itself. There are many social anthropologists who are no longer satisfied with mere correlations between institutions within a static structure, or system, but seek now to probe deeper into the processes of institutionalisation itself, into the underlying nature of obligation, into the all-pervading processes of symbolisation and hence of the dialectics of socio-cultural change. And this calls for the development of a more dynamic, more experimental, more analytical approach, than that of 'structural-functionalism' which has hitherto prevailed in one form or another.

The main obstacle to the development of such a dynamic approach is that during its formative years social anthropology was conceived in such a way as to make its methods and concepts applicable to the study of mainly 'primitive' societies. This was neatly summed up by Fortes (1953:38) in his inaugural lecture in Cambridge in 1952:

> The theoretically significant features of primitive societies are their homogeneity of culture, relative stability and lack of institutional differentiation. Wherever these characteristics occur together the theories and methods of social anthropology can be applied.

The implications for the study of complex society are obvious. As this society is culturally heterogeneous, continually changing, and institutionally differentiated, the theories and methods of social anthropology do not apply. This view fitted well with the evolutionary formulations of the great sociologists of the turn of the century, who saw a significant qualitative difference between the socio-cultural nature of primitive society and that of industrial complex society. Primitive society was said to be regulated by non-rational customs, while industrial society was said to be dominated by the rationality of bureaucracy. Social anthropology and sociology were branches of comparative sociology. The one was concerned with the sociology of primitive society; the other with the sociology of industrial society.

During the 1960s some anthropologists drew the obvious conclusions. Those of them who continued to be interested in the study of 'primitive' societies pursued the rapidly shrinking number of such societies, either by concentrating on the study of more remote and more isolated populations or by confining themselves to the 'traditional sector' of the less remote places, or by reconstructing the traditional past of such societies. Some of those who were interested in the study of complex society on the other hand opted out into sociology, and in the UK a number of these have eventually succeeded in capturing strategic chairs in sociology in the universities, often very much to the annoyance of the newly established sociologists. Other anthropologists have tended to avoid the theoretical issues involved by adopting the motto: 'we are all sociologists'.

But many others who for cne reason or another are committed to the social anthropological approach, and who are at the same time interested in the study of modern complex society, are now probing into the potentialities of their concepts and techniques for the study of contemporary industrial society.

This is of course not just a matter of labelling disciplines. Academically it will make little or no difference whether the analysis of socio-symbolic interdependence will be regarded as part of sociology or of political science or of social anthropology. The problem is much deeper than that. Social anthropology is not the sociology of primitive society any more than sociology is the social anthropology of modern society. Anthropologists specialise in the systematic observation and analysis of the drama of custom, or of symbolic behaviour generally. They pose major questions about man, society and culture, but seek to tackle these questions through intensive field work in small areas of social life and through rigorous comparative analysis developed in the course of extensive cumulative experience in the study of a variety of cultural codes in different parts of the world.

The first line for probing into the potentialities of social anthropology in the analysis of the dynamics of socio-symbolic phenomena in contemporary industrial society is to re-examine the major methodological and theoretical assumptions of this discipline in the light of nearly four decades of cumulative developments in both theory and subject-matter.

Outline of the argument

This will be discussed in the next two chapters which argue that the central theoretical problem in social anthropology has been the analysis of the dialectical relations between two major variables: symbolic action and power relationships. A concentration on the study of only one of these variables results in mere description. Only when the *relations* between the two domains are studied can significant analysis be made.

Chapter 4 deals with the nature of the obligatory, of the impelling 'ought', in symbolic action, in order to indicate the dialectical relation between the political on the one hand and the psychic and metaphysical on the other. Two sources of the obligatory that are common to both 'primitive' and industrial man are discussed. The first is the continuous struggle of man to achieve personal identity, or selfhood. The second is his concern with the perennial problems of human existence, like life and death, fortune and misfortune. On both fronts man resorts to symbolic action, in the course of which he continuously creates and recreates his oneness, and also develops solutions to the big, essentially irresolvable, questions of existence. Man is thus impelled to create symbols and to engage continuously in symbolic activities.

But individual creativity is limited and most men depend for the most part on the symbolic patterns given to them by the groups to which they belong and by society generally. These groups often manipulate not only the symbols that they hand over to the individual but also the intensity of man's 'need' for these symbols. For example, death, which poses a perennial problem for all men, is heavily symbolised and ceremonialised in some societies and much less so in others. In the one case it is highly dramatised, exaggerated and brought frequently to men's attention, while in others it is much less emphasised.

Chapter 5 shows how under certain structural circumstances some interest groups which cannot organise themselves as formal associations manipulate different forms of symbols in order to articulate informal organisational functions. Everywhere, Man the Symbolist and Man the Political act on one another. Often, different forms of symbols are exploited to achieve one organisational function and one form of symbols is exploited to articulate different organisational functions. The discussion covers both the basic organisational functions of interest groups and the various symbolic forms that are often exploited to articulate them.

The abstract formulations of the first five chapters are finally discussed in terms of ethnographic case studies in chapter 6. This concentration of documentation and illustration in a final part of the monograph, instead of spreading the material in the text, has been made in order to avoid giving haphazard, though plausible, 'apt illustrations' taken out of their context. For the benefit of general readers who are not familiar with abstract anthropological concepts and detailed ethnography, cross-references to the ethnographic cases are given in the earlier parts of the text. To ease the difficulty further, the following paragraphs give a brief survey of the cases.

All the cases cited are of interest groups that for some reason or another cannot organise themselves formally. The different types of cases are meant to demonstrate how different symbolic forms are adopted to articulate the same organisational functions under different conditions. First to be considered are interest groups that exploit ethnicity in their organisation in the contemporary situation. These groups manipulate values, myths, rituals and ceremonials from their cultural tradition to solve their basic organisational problems. To the casual observer ethnicity is taken as a manifestation of conservatism, separatism and stagnation, when on careful analysis we discover that it is a dynamic organisational mechanism involving intensive interaction with other groups. Ethnicity is shown to be essentially a political phenomenon.

Ethnicity is presented first, because it throws into relief, or rather dramatises, the more general, but less obvious, processes by which the symbolic patterns of behaviour implicit in the style of life, or the 'sub-culture', of a group develops to achieve basic organisational functions. This is shown in the contrasting case of the culture of the apparently highly individualistic groups of élites, with a particular attention to the business élite of the City of London. Here, the élite speak the same language and presumably partake in the same culture of the wider society, but when one looks closely into their style of life one will discover subtle peculiarities – in accent, manner of linguistic expression, style of dress, patterns of friendship and of marriage, etiquette, manners – that are organisationally instrumental in developing boundaries, communication, and other mechanisms for the organisation of the group. The élite thus co-ordinate their corporate activities through their style of life.

In the cases of both ethnicity and éliteness, different symbolic forms are combined to achieve the same organisational functions. In contrast, the third group of cases demonstrate the varied organisational potentialities of one symbolic form – religion. Here it is shown how religious beliefs, sentiments, rituals and organisation become also instrumental in co-ordinating the corporate organisation of interest groups.

This is followed by cases of articulation of informal organisation in terms of secret symbolic activities. A detailed case study of Freemasonry among the Creoles of Sierra Leone serves to indicate how highly privileged groups almost everywhere place great emphasis on 'privacy' as means of preventing general publics from discovering the organisational mechanisms that enable these groups to develop and maintain their privileged position. In all political systems, the men at the top develop a 'mystique' which raises them above the multitude, validates their status in the eyes of their publics and also convinces the men themselves of their own 'right' to their superior position in the society.

The final group of cases presented involve organisational articulation through the manipulation of female symbolism. In nearly all societies a number of roles and characteristics of womanhood are manipulated to develop the female image into one of the most potent symbols which is exploited in a variety of ways in the organisation of interest groups and in the struggle for power between them. An ideology which might originally be an essentially male creation is universalised and validated in terms of myths, values and norms that are inculcated, through continual socialisation, in the females of the society as well. Women bear children and thus affect recruitment to groups, are productive workers in the household or outside it, provide sexual pleasure for men, are usually entrusted with the socialisation of the young and can thus affect their sentiments, loyalties and style of life, ensure stable domestic and socio-cultural arrangements to enable males to be mobile, and in many places can hold property in their own right and can thus alienate it from men to men through inheritance. This multiplicity and complexity of values, contradictory meanings, sensuality and sentiments, and a host of other characteristics of womanhood have made it possible to transform the female 'mystique' into a powerful political symbol. The pattern of the movement of women in marriage in and between groups is intimately interconnected with the distribution of power in society. Relations of affinity established in one generation generate relationships of matrilaterality and patrilaterality in the next. The alliance established by the marriage becomes a cousinhood. The men become closely interrelated in a variety of ways. Three cases from different socio-cultural contexts are discussed. The first is of a small number of wealthy Anglo-Jewish families who started, at about the beginning of the nineteenth century, to exchange their women in marriage and thus developed within a few decades into a 'cousinhood alliance' which was used as an organisational mechanism in the efforts to remove the civic disabilities from which Jews suffered at the time. The next case shows how the Creoles of Sierra Leone developed a 'cousinhood network' – again through the exchange of women between families – which they use in the development and maintenance of their privileged position within Sierra Leone society. The final case demonstrates how in some Arab communities in Israel, the collectivity of men, who are manifestly organised as a patrilineage, is in fact an alliance created by a sustained pattern of marriage whereby the same men exchange a substantial proportion of their daughters and sisters in marriage. A whole cult of 'honour of women' is developed in the process as a mechanism for ensuring the maintenance of this pattern of marriage and hence of the interests that it serves. The same men become intensively linked and cross linked by patrilateral, matrilateral and affinal relationships.

In the conclusion, the discussion is brought to bear on the symbolism of power relationships in the large-scale modern industrial society generally. Classes are the figments of the imagination of sociologists. What actually exist are large numbers of interest groups of different scales and political significance, which can be ranged on one continuum, from the most formally organised to the most informally organised, with most of the groups falling in between, being partly formal and partly informal. Political anthropology specialises in unfolding the political implications of symbolic formations and activities – the 'mumbo-jumbo' of modern society – which are manifestly non-political, in the informal organisation of interest groups. It can thus make an important contribution to the social sciences in the systematic analysis of the dynamic processes involved in the institutionalisation and symbolisation of power relationships.

Power relations and symbolic action

2

The central theoretical issue in political anthropology
The power order
The symbolic order
Form and function of symbolic formations

Social stability was an essential heuristic condition for social structural analysis in the tradition of Durkheim and Radcliffe-Brown. A contemporaneous, holistic study of a society would make it possible to locate the contribution of an institution to the continuity and functioning of the whole of its structure. When stability was lacking – as indeed was the case with most of the communities studied – the anthropologist knowingly assumed its 'as if' existence (Gluckman 1968). In many cases the anthropologist concentrated on what he regarded as the 'traditional' part of a culture and lightly dismissed the rest under the heading of 'social change'. Change was seen as a nuisance, disturbing the neat pattern of the 'system'. In other cases the system was simply reconstructed on the basis of

18

documents and oral tradition. Anthropologists who for one reason or another did not like the term 'structure' operated with other terms like 'system' and 'equilibrium'.

But soon after the Second World War anthropologists began to realise that the study of 'society as a whole' was a vague and impractical proposition. In his now classic BBC talks on social anthropology, Evans-Pritchard (1951b) points out that anthropologists study problems, not peoples. The implication is that the anthropologist, like scientists in general, seeks to establish relations between sociocultural variables, and not to describe cultural items. Although Evans-Pritchard himself denied, in the same context, that social anthropology could ever be a natural science, he provided, at about the same time, one of the most brilliant analyses in social anthropology when he analysed the interdependence between politics and religion in his study of the Sanusi of Cyrenaica (1949). Holding constant other variables, like kinship and marriage, he analysed religio-political interdependence, showing step by step how changes in the one variable led to changes in the other. The Sanusi religious order succeeded in penetrating the political order of the tribes of Cyrenaica because it was carried by strangers who took no part in intei-tribal feuding. The tribes gave the Sanusis land and protection and the Sanusis provided the tribes with ritual services of all sorts. Then the whole population faced a serious threat to its existence when the Italians invaded the country. Because of the segmentary nature of the tribal structure the tribes needed a centralised political authority to mobilise the population for war and to co-ordinate its activities. But, as no such authority could arise out of the political order itself, the tribes turned to the Sanusis who, with their network of local lodges and centralised ritual authority, had the means of providing channels for communication between the various parts of the population, leadership, ideology and mechanisms for decision-making. The hitherto purely ritual order became highly politicised. In its turn the order reacted on the political structure of the tribes, changing it from a segmentary polity to a centralised one. The ritual order and the political structure of the tribes became one, and their unity came to be symbolised by the ritual head of the order, who eventually was to become the king of the whole country. This politico-ritual interdependence was so strong, that in order to crush the tribes, the Italians had to crush the order. In the final stages they sought to capture the Sanusi and to crown him officially as king, in order to dethrone him and thereby symbolise the destruction of the political resistance movement.

This and some other studies on similar lines have demonstrated that what we mean by system is not a 'holistic', organic, entity, but a number of socio-cultural variables that are interrelated in specific ways. This means that in order to study how two, or more, of these variables are interrelated, you will have to proceed in the same way as other scientists proceed: change one variable and, keeping the other variables constant, observe the concomitant changes in another variable. This is indeed the 'experimental method' in a nutshell. But while the natural scientist can often perform experiments in the laboratory for observation, this is not possible for the anthropologist, for whom, instead, two alternatives are open. The first is the comparative method. But mainly because of the multiplicity of variables involved in each socio-cultural system and of the complexity of the ways in which these variables are interrelated in the different systems, the difficulties in isolating variables and analysing their interdependence by comparison alone are many.

The second alternative, which has been used in combination with the first, is the study of change in one socio-cultural system. Those who have been influenced by the structural-functional approach accommodated this method within their conceptual scheme by the synchronic, cross-sectional study of the same system at different points in historical time (see, for example, Gluckman 1942; Smith 1960; Cohen 1965). As a good deal of continuity of many variables between one historical stage and another occurred, it has been possible, by comparing the different stages, to isolate variables in a far more satisfactory manner than in the comparison between different societies, with different cultural traditions that were studied by different anthropologists. But even this second alternative assumed 'as if' stability in the analysis of each one of the different stages. Nevertheless, this marked an important advance.

But if we indeed study problems, not peoples, then we have to operate in terms of variables. Socio-cultural change will then be heuristically a necessity, not a hindrance. It will provide us with empirical situations in which it will be possible to see how change in one variable leads to change in another, with the other variables remaining constant. As we shall in this way be dealing with socio-cultural causation and interdependence, we shall ultimately be able to study the process of institutionalisation, or of symbolisation itself. We shall thus avoid a good deal of conjectural formulations based on mechanical correlations between variables in a static, contemporaneous, synchronic system.

The central theoretical issue in political anthropology

Social anthropology is essentially concerned with the dialectical relation between two major variables: symbolic action and power relationships. A discipline is defined in terms of the major problems with which it deals. A 'problem' in this context refers to a gap existing in our knowledge about the way in which variables are related to one another. The advance of a discipline is as much in the identification and isolation of these variables as in the analysis of their interdependence. As Homans once pointed out, one of the lessons we learn from the older sciences is to cut down, as far as we dare, the number of the variables with which we deal.

The first major theoretical and methodological breakthrough in the development of social anthropology occurred when Durkheim, and later Radcliffe-Brown, advocated the analytical isolation of social from historical and from psychological 'facts'. It is true that in recent years this has been subjected to criticism by some anthropologists, on a variety of grounds. But this criticism has so far been directed against the rigidity, not the theoretical principles, underlying this separation. Even those anthropologists who regard social anthropology as a kind of historiography and call for the analysis of historical data by anthropologists agree, nevertheless, that social institutions cannot be sociologically *explained* in terms of past origins or events (Evans-Pritchard 1956:60). Similarly, even in the study of the symbols and of symbolic behaviour, whose operation is closely involved in psychic processes, the separation of the social from the psychic has been systematically maintained (Leach 1958; Gluckman 1963; 1968; Turner 1964).

Following the theoretical leads by Durkheim and Radcliffe-Brown, social anthropologists developed the so-called 'holistic' approach to society and concentrated on the study of what came to be known as 'social structure'. But, setting aside explicit theoretical and methodological formulations, the question should be asked: what have social anthropologists actually done in order to study the social structure holistically? The answer can be found in the monographic studies which they have produced.

Broadly speaking, social anthropologists have interpreted the 'holism' of the social structure in terms of a limited number of specific institutions (Beattie 1959). A survey of the monographs will show that they have generally concentrated on the study of four broad institutional spheres: economic, political, kinship and ritual. On a higher level of abstraction these four institutional spheres can be classified into two categories. The political and the economic form one category, their common denominator being power relationships. Kinship and religion form the second category, their common denominator being symbolism. As I show below, these two categories of institutions represent two major variables that for brevity I shall call 'the political' and 'the symbolic'.

The power order

The separation between the economic and the political in socio-anthropological studies is often very arbitrary. What has come to be known as 'economic anthropology' is in fact an admixture of descriptions of two different kinds of phenomena: economic *process* and economic *relationships*. These two features of economic activity have been analysed within two different conceptual schemes that have been developed by two different disciplines. Economic process refers to the interaction between man and the relatively scarce resources available to him. It is a part of technology. Economic relationships, on the other hand, refer to interaction between man and man in the course of the economic process. Social anthropologists have been interested principally in economic relationships, i.e. in relationships between individuals and groups in the processes of production, exchange and distribution, and most social anthropologists who paid attention to process have done so mainly in so far as process affected economic relationships.

But as Marx and others have indicated, these economic relationships are relations of power and are thus essentially political, forming a major part of the political order in any society. Nearly everywhere in simple societies the system of land tenure, client-patron relationships, exchange and the distribution of goods are inseparable parts of the political order. In many centralised tribal societies, the king or chief 'owns the land' as a trustee and allocates it to the people who have the right to its use. This, in turn, entitles him to demand allegiance from the people. In many uncentralised societies, mythologies of kinship, that are often articulated in the form of elaborate genealogies, regulate the distribution of land and political groupings at one and the same time. Similarly, in the advanced industrial societies the relationships between property owner and user, employer and employee, producer and consumer, and a host of similar relationships are maintained and regulated by the laws of the state. Economic interests and political interests interpenetrate each other and act and react on one another. They continually exert pressure on the state and the state continually exerts pressure on them.

This is not to maintain that these two types of power, the economic and the political, are indistinguishable one from the other. They certainly differ in a number of respects. The relationships which they govern are formally regulated by different mechanisms. Political power is ultimately maintained by physical coercion. Economic power is ultimately maintained by reward and deprivation. They are nevertheless intimately interconnected and, in many contexts, inseparable. In both, we are in fact dealing with relationships of power between individuals and groups, when these relationships are considered structurally throughout the extent of a polity. In both institutions relationships are manipulative, technical, contractual and instrumental, as men in different situations use one another as means to ends and not as ends in themselves.

The symbolic order

Similarly, the institutions of kinship and ritual, though distinct in form, have a great deal in common, and the separation between them is often arbitrary and sometimes misleading. They are both normative, governed by categorical imperatives, or 'oughts', that are rooted in the psychic structure of men in society through continuous socialisation. A man respects his father because he 'ought' to do so, irrespective of any utilitarian considerations. In a similar fashion, a man 'ought' to worship God. Both institutions operate by means of symbolic formations and symbolic activities.

Symbols are objects, acts, relationships or linguistic formations that stand *ambiguously* for a multiplicity of meanings, evoke emotions, and impel men to action. They usually occur in stylised

23

patterns of activities, such as ritual, ceremonial, gift exchange, prescribed patterns of joking, taking an oath, eating and drinking together, acts of etiquette, and various culture traits that constitute the style of life of a group. A symbol is contrasted with a sign. A road sign, such as a red circle on white background with the figure '70' in it, can only mean for the driver one thing: that the speed limit is 70 m.p.h. A shape like the cross on the other hand holds different meanings to different persons and to the same person at different times. A sign need not agitate feelings but a symbol does.

The difference between a sign and a symbol is a matter of degree, depending on the density of different and disparate meanings that it connotes, on the intensity of feelings that it evokes, and on its action-impelling properties. This variation in degree can be described as 'potency', and symbols can be ranged on one continuum from the least potent, a mere sign, to the most potent, a 'dominant symbol' (Turner 1964; 1968) or a 'significant symbol' (Duncan 1968).

Symbols tend to be grouped together within the frameworks of dynamic ideologies, or world-views, that are developed and carried by specific groupings. In these ideologies the symbols of inter-personal relationships, like kinship and friendship, are integrated with those of ritual, which deal with such perennial problems of human existence as the meaning of life and death, illness and health, misery and happiness, fortune and misfortune. These two symbolic complexes support one another within the ideology and are made to express and validate the political organisation of these groupings.

Both categories of symbols, those of kinship and of ritual, have been used almost interchangeably in the articulation of political groupings and of power relationships between individuals and groups. Ritual symbols form part of most kinship systems, and kinship symbols form part of most ritual systems. Kinship symbols are said to be particularly suited to articulate cyclically changing interpersonal relationships, while ritual symbols are said to be particularly suited to express political relations of a higher level. But there are many cases where a kinship ideology is made to articulate the political organisation of large populations in both uncentralised and centralised societies. The Bedouin of Cyrenaica (Peters 1960; 1967) and the Tallensi (Fortes 1945; 1949), for example, express their political organisation in the idiom of kinship. The same can be said of the organisation of kingdoms. The whole political structure of the Swazi is expressed in a lineage pattern that pervades the whole kingdom from the highest to the lowest levels (Kuper 1947). In other centralised societies kinship symbols articulate political groupings and political relations on only some levels. Among the Mambwe (Watson 1958) and the Lunda of the Luapula valley (Cunnison 1959) the stability of the political structure at the top is symbolised in terms of 'perpetual kinship' relationships. Among the Ashanti, on the other hand, only the lower part of the political structure is organised on a kinship basis (Fortes 1950). But even when we consider the symbolism of interpersonal relationships in large-scale, contemporary industrial society, we can see that these symbols articulate an endless array of informal political groupings whose operation is a fundamental part of the total political structure of the society.

Similarly, ritual symbols need not be exclusively involved in the articulation of the relatively high level, large-scale, political groupings, and can be seen to express various types of interpersonal relationships. Thus, as Gluckman (1962) points out, in most tribal societies, interpersonal relationships are highly 'ritualised'. Also, in many Mediterranean and Latin American countries extensive use is made of the ritual kinship relationships created by the institution of 'god-parenthood', *Compadrazgo*, in the organisation of various types of interpersonal relationships and of groupings, in some cases between the socially equal, in others between the socially unequal (Mintz and Wolf 1950, 1956; Pitt-Rivers 1958; Deshon 1963; Osborn 1968; Gudeman 1972).

Kinship symbols and ritual symbols are highly interdependent and neither category can operate without the other. The distinction between them is often based, not on objective sociological analysis, but on native usages and ideologies. The same can be said of the broader distinction between 'sacred symbols' and 'profane symbols', or between ritual and ceremonial generally (Leach 1954:13; Martin 1965; Douglas 1966:65).

This is not to say that there are no significant differences between symbols, or that symbols should not be categorised. But symbols are highly complex socio-cultural phenomena and can be classified according to a variety of criteria, depending on the purpose of the classification. In other words, such a classification depends on the nature of the problem being investigated and on the variables that are considered in the study. In social anthropology the central theoretical interest in the study of symbols is the analysis of their involvement in the relationships of power, and this will call for a type of classification which may often be at variance with that provided by the cultural traditions of which the symbols are part.

Form and function of symbolic formations

It is essential that we distinguish between symbolic *forms* and symbolic *functions*. The same symbolic function, within a particular political context, can be achieved by a variety of symbolic forms. For example, every political group must have symbols of distinctiveness, i.e. of identity and exclusiveness defining its boundaries. But this can be achieved in different symbolic forms: emblems, facial markings, myths of origin, customs of endogamy or of exogamy, beliefs and practices associated with the ancestors, genealogies, specific ceremonials, special styles of life, shrines, notions of purity and pollution, and so on (Cohen 1969b:201–14). Thus, ritual symbols and kinship symbols may differ in form but not necessarily in function.

It is also important to remember that these two forms of symbols do not exhaust between them the whole symbolic universe in a society. There are many other forms of symbols that are not ordinarily subsumed under either the category of kinship or ritual. This is such an obvious point that it seems unnecessary to mention it. Yet it is surprising how often we tend to forget it and thus lead ourselves astray in our observation and analysis. This is particularly the case when we study changing pre-industrial societies or more developed societies. Often in such cases traditional symbols of kinship and of ritual lose their significance and we then begin to talk of 'social disintegration' or, when we refer to ritual particularly, of 'secularisation'. It then becomes easy to slip into the theoretical position that the hold of symbols on social relationships is weakening as the society becomes more socially differentiated and more formally and rationally organised.

The continuity, ubiquity and intensity of symbolic forms and symbolic action in contemporary, complex society has been ignored or minimised by some writers for a number of reasons, of which two are particularly relevant to the present discussion.

The first is the tendency to turn symbolic forms into sociological fetishes. Social anthropologists have been interested in religion and kinship, as these have figured prominently in the organisation of pre-industrial societies. In due course they became so intrigued by these that they have turned them into a major preoccupation. The complaint by some scholars about the obsession of social anthropologists with 'kinship algebra', for example, is not unjustified in some cases. Indeed with some anthropologists the study of kinship forms has become an end in itself, thus turning an idiom underlying the dynamic processes of interpersonal interaction into an object of abstract and sociologically sterile analysis. This obsession with forms has been so strong that when in the 1950s scholars like Willmott and Young (1957) 'rediscovered' the extended family in British society there was great excitement among some scholars, a number of whom hurried to apply themselves energetically to fill this gap in our knowledge. What they found, in one study after another, was that kin in some cases still co-operate in baby-minding, in some domestic tasks and, in some few cases, in finding jobs and accommodation.

What is astonishing is that some scholars should attach so much significance to these relics of kinship relationships and turn a myopic eye on the extensive networks of other kinds of interpersonal relationships that fulfil the same functions and that have not yet been fully identified and analysed. I have known closely for a number of years a community which developed on a new middle-class housing estate in a London suburb. It consisted mainly of spiralist families, the families of business executives who were rapidly rising in status and hence also geographically mobile. The families were relatively young, mostly with young children. Husbands tended to be absent in remote places of work in the city, leaving their homes from the early hours of the morning until late in the evening. Many of them had to entertain customers in town after finishing office hours. Some of them travelled extensively on business missions either within the country or abroad and were thus absent from their families, sometimes for weeks. Thus wives were left alone to cope with the children, with shopping, and with household work. Only a few of the families were locals. Some of these interacted with their parents, siblings, or first cousins. These families, particularly when the wives had cars at their disposal, tended to have many of their social contacts outside the estate. But the rest of the families, who formed the overwhelming majority of the estate community, were strangers. An intensive study of these

27

families (Cohen, E. G., 1973), however, reveals that these non-local wives soon managed to have the same kind of help that the local wives were getting from their kin. In the course of only a few months after settlement began in the estate, several groupings of such wives were formed. The members of such groups established patterns of co-operation in shopping, baby-minding, taking children to school, baby-sitting in the evenings, organising play groups, entertaining the children on birthdays. Indeed some of the local wives found these arrangements more satisfactory than those making use of kin, or when kin were of a lower social status than the couple who were too sensitive to introduce them to their neighbours. These relationships of co-operation on the estate soon became institutionalised and duly validated by new patterns of symbolic behaviour: coffee sessions, gift exchanges, interdining, visiting, participation in the rites of passage. A new 'culture' thus developed and took shape. This 'culture' soon became an 'objective' entity existing in its own right. As the families were mobile, some families that were initially involved in the formation of this culture moved away. The new-comers who replaced these in their houses came to find an already existing culture 'handed over' to them, maintaining specific types of co-operation. They immediately found out that in order to par-take in the network of co-operation they had to abide by the norms and ceremonials supporting it.

There must be millions of families in the UK and the USA who take part in similar networks of relationships that are regulated by similar cultures. The proportion of those who continue to make use of traditional kinship relationships must be insignificant compared with these networks. Indeed, what is sociologically significant is not that a little extended kinship still exists and operates here and there in modern society, but how much co-operation is effected through entirely new patterns of relationships. It is these new patterns, not the traditional ones, that represent a challenge to the sociological imagination. These 'cultures' of contemporary families have not yet been sufficiently identified or explored. Indeed, the whole field of friendship in modern society remains enveloped in mystery. It is no exaggeration to say that we know more about friendship in pre-industrial societies than in developed societies, where it plays a far more fundamental role in social organisation.

In a similar manner, sociologists and anthropologists find every-where in modern society the dwindling importance of formal religion, but fail to identify and probe into new patterns of symbolic action that replace the old ones in fulfilling old as well as new structural functions. The numerous patterns of ceremonials that pervade our life on all levels of social organisation do not figure prominently in sociological literature. The sociological functions of the symbolic dramas that are staged to us daily on television, radio, in the cinema and on the pages of other mass media of communication have been little touched by students of socio-cultural phenomena (for a recent attempt here see Goodlad 1971). The same can be said of such exotic phenomena as the horoscope in the popular daily and weekly papers, of voodoo, psychic research, spiritual healings, witchcraft practices, and a host of other phenomena. It is only recently that some beginnings have been made, principally by social anthropologists, in scratching into the symbolic significance of different forms of mass entertainment like football and dancing, which figure so prominently in social life in large-scale societies (see Mitchell 1956; Frankenberg 1957; Gluckman (forthcoming); Banton 1957). Thus, although kinship symbols and ritual symbols may become obsolete in modern society, other symbols take their place in articulating old, as well as new, symbolic functions. A change of symbolic form does not automatically entail a change of symbolic function, because the same function can be achieved by new forms. Similarly, a continuity of symbolic form need not automatically entail a continuity of symbolic function for the same form can fulfil new functions. In some situations old symbols are revived to perform new functions (Gluckman 1942; Cohen 1965). The challenge to social anthropology today is the analysis of this dynamic involvement of symbols, or of custom, in the changing relationships of power between individuals and groups.

Societies often adopt different symbolic forms to achieve the same kind of symbolic functions. This is what we mean by cultural differences. These differences arise as a result of different combinations of circumstances, some of which can be historical, cultural and ecological. Some symbolic forms are adopted from other peoples through interaction with them at different historical periods; others are conditioned by special factors. For example, a people living in a forest area will make use of trees in carving symbols, or in general symbolic representation, while a people living in the desert will make use of other media and experiences in constructing their symbolic forms. Again, because Islam is categorically opposed to the employment of painting, carving, dancing and music in the construction of its ritual symbols, extensive use is made in orthodox Islamic countries of a wide range of linguistic forms – rhetoric, proverbs and the like.

Symbolic forms are the products of creative work. Their internal structure is a dramatic structure and their study is partly a study in the sociology of art. Many symbols are the creation of anonymous artists. It is mainly in more advanced and sophisticated literate societies that special, named artists are commissioned to create symbols for specific functions – to design a flag, write an anthem, compose music for a hymn, paint a picture of a saint, stage a ceremonial. But we are all potential creators of symbols (see Leach 1954:14–15). Through our dreams, illusions, spontaneous activities, moments of reflection and in the general flow of our consciousness, we continually proliferate symbols and manipulate them. Many men keep their symbolic creativity to themselves. Others externalise it and try to share their symbols with other men. This symbolic proliferation within each one of us is not entirely our autonomous creation, but is the product of a dialectical interaction between ourselves and our social reality. At times of change, some men's symbolic forms can provide better solutions to the current problems of a group than other symbols and those men who articulate them may become leaders and have their symbols adopted by the group. There is thus a great deal of the creative artist in the political leader who, through his rhetoric, slogans and tactics, manipulates existing symbols or creates new ones. When this creativity is particularly original, when it helps to articulate or to objectify new groupings and new relationships, we describe him as 'charismatic'.

Social anthropologists analyse symbolic forms in order to discover their symbolic functions. One of the most important of these functions is the objectification of relationships between individuals and groups. We can observe individuals objectively in concrete reality, but the relationships between them are abstractions that can be observed only through symbols. Social relationships develop through and are maintained by symbols. We 'see' groups through their symbols. Values, norms, rules and abstract concepts like honour, prestige, rank, justice, good and evil are made tangible through symbols, and men in society are thus helped to be aware of their existence, to comprehend them and to relate them to their daily life.

Symbols also objectify roles and give them a reality which is separate from the individual personalities of their incumbents. Men are trained for their roles, installed in them, and helped to perform their duties in the course of a series of stylised symbolic activities. By objectifying relations and roles, symbols help to differentiate between them, a function particularly important in the context of multiplex relationships (Gluckman 1962), i.e. relationships which serve different interests between the same individuals.

By objectifying roles and relations, symbolism achieves a measure of stability and continuity without which social life cannot exist. Power is an erratic process. A vengeance group such as a lineage in some societies may have to wait for years before it finds itself involved in a case of homicide that will require action on the part of all of its members. But it must be ready for action all the time; for such an event can occur at any moment. Its members cannot afford to disband in the meantime, but must keep their grouping alive. This continuity of the group can be achieved mainly through group symbolism, not through the irregular exercise of power by the whole group. Similarly, although a regime may come to office and maintain itself for some time by sheer force, its stability and continuity are achieved mainly through the symbolism of authority which it manipulates. Subjects do not start their lives every morning examining the dispositions of power in their society to see whether the regime is still backed by the same amount of force as before, or whether that force has diminished and the regime can therefore be overthrown. The stability and continuity of the regime are made possible through a complex system of symbolism that gives it legitimacy by representing it ultimately as a 'natural' part of the universe.

Through the 'mystification' which they create, symbols make it possible for the social order to survive the disruptive processes created within it by the inevitable areas of conflicting values and principles. It does this by creating communion between potential enemies. A proverb among Arab peasants states: 'I against my brother; I and my brother against our cousin; I and my brother and my cousin against the outsider.' A man discovers his identity through interaction with others. To co-operate with his brother against their cousin he must reconcile his hostility to his brother with the need to identify with him in the fight against their cousin.

He, his brother, and their cousin must achieve communion to contain their enmities if they are to co-operate against the common enemy.

As Smith points out (1956), all politics, all struggle for power, is segmentary. This means that enemies at one level must be allies at a different level. Thus a man is forced to be an enemy and an ally with the same set of people, and it is mainly through the 'mystification' generated by symbolism that these contradictions are repetitively faced and temporarily resolved. Indeed, Gluckman (1963:18) goes so far in elaborating on this function of symbols as to state that ritual and ceremonial do not simply express cohesion and impress the value of society and its social sentiments on people, as in Durkheim's and Radcliffe-Brown's theories, but exaggerate real conflicts of social rules and affirm that there is unity despite these conflicts.

The degree of 'mystification', and of the potency of the dominant symbols that are employed to create it, mounts as the conflict, contradiction, or inequality between people who should identify in communion increases. This is a point stressed and greatly illuminated by Marx in his exposure of the mysteries of capitalist symbols and 'ideologies'. It is further elaborated and discussed by Duncan (1962) who points out that all social order involves hierarchy, that all hierarchy involves relations between superiors, inferiors and equals, and that relationships between these are developed and maintained through the 'mystification' of the symbolism of communion. These and many other functions tend to be achieved, at one and the same time, by the same symbolic formations. The same symbol can contribute to the accomplishment of selfhood, objectification, continuity, communion, as well as some such organisational functions as distinctiveness, communication, authority, ideology and discipline. It is indeed in the very essence of the symbolic process to perform a multiplicity of functions with economy of symbolic formation. The more meanings a symbol signifies, the more ambiguous and flexible it becomes, the more intense the feelings that it evokes, the greater its potency, and the more functions it achieves.

It is not my intention to attempt to give here a survey of the various symbolic functions that have been analysed by social anthropologists. Many such functions have been identified and explored. But the systematic search for them and the analysis of the ways in which these functions do their job is still at its beginning. What I want to stress is that social anthropologists have been collectively concerned with the analysis of symbols in contexts of power relationships.

Although anthropologists have *individually* differed in their interests, approaches and explanations in the analysis of symbolic forms and functions, they have *collectively* been concerned with the interdependence between symbolism and power relationships.

There is nothing theoretically radical in this statement. Some of the leading social anthropologists have expressed the same view, though often using different terms. Thus Leach (1954:14) maintains that the main task of social anthropology is to interpret symbolic statements and actions in terms of social relations. Similarly, Gluckman (1942) and Fortes (1953) have for a long time held the view that social anthropology differs from the other social sciences in that it is concerned with customs, which, when considered on a higher level of abstraction, are essentially what I am calling symbols. I find the term 'social relations', which we often use in such formulations, to be vague and imprecise. It is a blank term which encompasses so many things that it in effect refers only to a universe of discourse and not to anything specific within that universe. It implicitly contains, among other things, the symbols that express and maintain the relationships. The term 'power relations' on the other hand is more precise, representing only one aspect of social relations. On a high level of abstraction all social relationships have their aspect of power. Power, as many scholars have pointed out, does not exist in the abstract but always inheres in social relationships.

This does not mean that all social anthropologists are in agreement that they are principally concerned with the study of the symbolism of power relations. As we shall see below, a few of them are barely interested in the study of symbols and concentrate on the study of power relations and power struggles between individuals and groups. Other social anthropologists, on the other hand, are not interested in the study of relations of power and concentrate on the study of symbols as such. But the overwhelming majority of social anthropologists fall on the continuum between these two extremes in that their work consists in the analysis of various types of symbols within essentially political contexts. Often they alternate in their analysis between these two variables, though some do so more consciously, explicitly and systematically than others.

The two variables are in fact two broad aspects of nearly all social behaviour. As Nadel (1951:28–9) and Goffman (1969) have shown, all social behaviour is couched in symbolic forms. Relationships of friendship, kinship and affinity, patron-client, ruler and subject, elder and junior, and many others that make up the vast network of relations between men and groups in society, all these relationships are seen in stylised forms of symbolic behaviour that constitute the phenomenological flow of social life. On the other hand relations of power are aspects of nearly all social relationships. This holds true of even so-called domestic relations, which some social anthropologists seem to exclude from the realm of politics. Relations like those between father and son, or husband and wife, have their own aspects of power and thus form part of the political order in any society. Thus, in the words of Leach (1954:13): 'Technique and ritual, profane and sacred, do not denote types of action but *aspects* of almost any kind of action.'

There is no assumption here that these two aspects account exhaustively for all concrete social behaviour; for this is a highly complex process which cannot be reduced to the operation of a few variables. Power relationships and symbolic behaviour are only analytically isolated from concrete social behaviour, in order to study the sociological relations between them.

The dialectics of politico-symbolic interdependence

Continuity and change in symbolic formations
Action theorists (or transactionalists)
Thought structuralists
Analysis v. description in social science

Power relations and symbolic formations are not reducible one to the other. Each is qualitatively different from the other, having its own characteristics and its own form of process. They are relatively autonomous orders. Symbols are not the mechanical reflections, or representations, of political realities. People worship, seek entertainment with one another, exchange gifts, partake in ceremonial and get married for a variety of private motives. But their activities in these respects have political consequences that can be discovered by sociological analysis. A prayer is an intrinsic value in its own right. So is marriage. It is therefore absurd to talk of a 'political prayer' or of a 'political marriage'. It is legitimate, however, to talk about the political aspects of a prayer or the political aspects of marriage, in order to indicate that the prayer or the marriage, though being an institution in its own right, is involved in and affected by political relations. Hence our discussion of 'the politics of marriage' or 'the politics of ceremonial'. Symbolic formations thus have an existence of their own, in their own right, and can affect power relations in a variety of ways. Similarly, power relations have a reality of their own and can in no way be said to be determined by symbolic categories. If the one variable were an exact reflection of the other, then the study of their interdependence would be of little sociological value. It is only because they are different, yet interdependent, that their isolation and the study of the relations between them can be fruitful and illuminating.

Though autonomous, the political and the symbolic are interdependent in such a way that a change in the one is likely to affect the relation between the two even if the other remains apparently unchanged. For example, a change in power relationships may not lead to a change in the form of kinship. But in the new situation the idiom of kinship will assume different functions. *Socio-cultural causation operates dialectically, not mechanically.*

Continuity and change in symbolic formations

On the whole, symbolic formations and patterns of action tend to persist longer than power relationships in changing socio-cultural systems. The universality of the problems of selfhood, of man's place in the universe, of the structure of authority, and of a host of other fields in social life that will be discussed in detail in the following chapters, inevitably lead to cultural or symbolic continuities amidst even the most radical political changes. But there are other processes involved in this 'conservative' nature of culture which should be taken into consideration in the analysis of socio-cultural interdependence, that pertain to the nature of the symbolic order itself.

The first point that stands out immediately is the general flexibility of symbolic forms. One of the major characteristics of symbolic formations is their multiplicity of meaning. The same symbolic form may have different shades of meaning to different individuals, and at different times to the same individual. It is given to different interpretations by different people and under different circumstances. A symbol will not do its work if it did not have this ambiguity and flexibility. Indeed it is this very flexibility that ensures a measure of continuity of social organisation. Social life is highly dynamic, continuously changing and if the symbols associated with these relations change erratically there will be no order, and life will be chaotic and impossible. As Berger and Luckman (1967:121) put it:

> *All* social reality is precarious. *All* societies are constructions in the face of chaos. The constant possibility of anomic terror is actualized whenever the legitimations that obscure the precariousness are threatened or collapse.

And Gluckman (1955) pointed out in relation to legal norms that there is nothing more fatal to social organisation than too precise definitions of terms. It is only thanks to this flexibility of symbols that a measure of ordered social life is possible. Symbols are continuously interpreted and reinterpreted. Duncan (1969:7–8) points out that:

> it is the ambiguity of symbols which makes them so useful in human society. Ambiguity is a kind of bridge that allows us to run back and forth from one kind of meaning to another, until we take firm resolve to cross the bridge into new, and fixed, meanings.

This means that minor or temporary changes in the relations of power need not be immediately accommodated by corresponding changes in the symbolic forms.

Related to this is the fact that when such relationships between individuals change, this change will be part of their personal biographies and will not be immediately validated by changes in the symbolic structure. As Berger and Luckman (1967) show, the need for such a change will occur only when a second generation, or newcomers, will step into the structure. Symbolic validation will then become necessary.

A third process results from the tendency in all groupings for the different parts of the symbolic order to form an integrated system, an ideology or world-view whose general form exerts pressure, so to speak, on the parts. Institutionalisation occurs only when a practice becomes somehow accommodated within this symbolic system. A pattern of marriage for example will become institutionalised when it becomes adjusted to the economic, political, and religious institutions of the society. It has been repeatedly pointed out by many scholars that institutions tend to hang together. Often a change in only one institution, or one type of power relation, will not lead to an immediate corresponding change of the whole symbolic structure. On the other hand, when as a result of political upheavals a new symbolic system, like a religion, or a comprehensive political ideology is adopted, the whole system will be accepted even if parts of it do not fit the political relations. In time slow adjustments take place.

A fourth process is related to the life-span of some major symbolic forms. The pattern of marriage for example has everywhere been part of the symbolic order validating the distribution of power in a society. A sudden political change will not be immediately followed by scrapping and reorganising the distribution or circulation of women and children. Most of the existing marriages that were contracted under the old conditions will continue to run their full courses under the new circumstances. What is more, there is always the tendency for such a 'lag' to be incorporated within the new order of things if it can be reinterpreted and given new functions and new values.

Indeed it is this very 'conservative' characteristic of theirs that makes symbolic formations so fundamental for the establishment and continuity of social order. One of the contradictions of social change is that it is effected through continuities. Even the most radical political revolutions will accept and continue to implement the bulk of the body of laws governing civil life that it inherits from the displaced regime. A great deal of the symbolic order of the older regime will continue to exist, as otherwise life will be so chaotic that the whole social order will disintegrate and the revolution will collapse in chaos. In our own time this seems to be the lesson of the cultural revolution in China. According to Marxian doctrine every economic order is validated and supported by a 'superstructure', what I have called a symbolic order. After the communist revolution in Russia a great deal of the pre-revolutionary 'superstructure', of 'bourgeois' cultural traits, survived and were duly accommodated within the new politico-symbolic system. The Chinese communists, after the success of their revolution, attacked this 'reaction' on the part of the Russian communist regime. They subsequently sought to eradicate all 'bourgeois' and conservative elements of the pre-revolutionary superstructure in their society. But in the attempt the whole structure of Chinese society was being undermined and for about two years the country seemed to be heading towards anarchy. Eventually this threatened the revolution itself and the leaders of the cultural revolution had to call off their assault (see Robinson 1969).

It is possible to change power relationship in a society overnight, but a great deal of the symbols validating and supporting those relationships will survive and will change only slowly. This continuity of symbolic forms however does not entail automatically the continuity of the same functions that those symbols performed in the past. In the new situation the old symbolic forms may perform new functions. Thus as I show in the analysis of some cases in chapter 6, there are situations in contemporary Afiica and the USA for example in which many culture groups – tribes, or ethnic groups – not only retain but also exaggerate their traditional culture. To the casual observer this seems to be a manifestation of social conservatism and reaction, but a careful analysis shows that the old symbols are rearranged to serve new purposes under new political conditions. In ethnicity, old symbols and ideologies become strategies for the articulation of new interest groupings that struggle for employment, housing, funds and other new benefits. In Northern Ireland old religious symbols are used in a violent struggle over economic and political issues within the contemporary situation.

It is this lack of mechanical 'fitness' between the symbolic order and the power order that makes socio-cultural change such a significant field of study. For it presents the social scientist with situations in which old symbolic forms perform new symbolic functions and new symbolic forms perform old symbolic functions. The detailed analysis of this dialectical process will shed substantial light on the processes of symbolisation and institutionalisation. Ultimately, such analysis will enable us to probe into the nature of politico-symbolic causation generally.

Analysis in social anthropology has consisted in the study of interdependence, or of dialectical interaction, between the two variables rather than in the study of either of the variables separately. A concentration on only one, to the neglect of the other, will result mainly in descriptions whose theoretical value will be limited. This is of course a bald statement, for each of the two variables contains 'sub-variables' whose operation and interdependence must be analysed to make our description of the major variable more refined and more accurate. The difference between analysis and description is a matter of degree.

There are at present two experimental trends in social anthropology, each of which is concerned principally with only one of the two major variables.

Action theorists (or transactionalists)

The one trend is a reaction against the emphasis placed by earlier anthropological studies on 'collective representations' in the classical Durkheimian tradition. This school of thought tends to sweep the theoretical pendulum towards the orientation emanating from the Weberian 'action theory' (see P. S. Cohen 1968). This theoretical approach (see, for example, Barth 1966; 1967; Boissevain 1968; Mayer 1966; Nicholas 1965) distrusts analysis in terms of groups and of group symbols, and concentrates on the activities of 'political man' who is ever impelled to the pursuit of power. Mayer (1966:119) states in a cautious way: 'It may well be that, as social anthropologists become more interested in complex societies and as the simpler societies themselves become more complex, an increasing amount of work will be based on ego-centred entities such as action sets and quasi-groups, rather than on groups and subgroups.' In a recent article Boissevain (1968:544–5) pushes this position to its limit: 'The accent must shift from the *group* towards the *individual*. . . . Individuals, and the loose coalitions they form are thus logically prior to groups and society. A view which postulates the reverse is illogical.'

Anthropologists of this school of thought present a picture of political life in terms of a continuing 'game', in which every man is seeking to maximise his power by perpetually scheming, struggling, and making decisions. Every action he contemplates is the outcome of a transaction in which the returns are expected to be at least equal to, if not in excess of, the outlay.

Action theory anthropologists have deepened our understanding of the dynamic processes involved in the struggle for power that goes on, not only within changing societies, but also within traditional societies. They have used a 'microscope' to show us politics at the grass-roots level, and have introduced into our vocabulary a number of valuable terms to label 'non-group' collectivities: 'faction', 'egocentric network', 'action set'. Bailey (1969) presents and discusses a body of concepts and terms designed to deal, in a very perceptive and penetrating way, with the subtleties of political behaviour at this level. These concepts and terms direct our attention to types of groupings and to processes of political inter- action that have so far escaped our attention, and thus provide us with important tools, not only for analysis but also for the collection of field data.

But when this orientation is pushed to its extreme and is pre- sented, as Boissevain (1968) does, as a substitute for the 'old methods', it becomes one-sided and thus gives a distorted picture of socio-cultural reality. To put it metaphorically, the microscope that this school holds is so powerful in disclosing the details of face-to-face political interaction that it is powerless, or out of focus, to reflect the wider structural features of society.

Boissevain is certainly right in stating that the individual is prior to the group, but only if he is referring to the *biological* individual. In society, however, we do not deal with biological individuals but with social personalities. The greater part of our 'human nature' is acquired from society through socialisation. As G. H. Mead (1934) shows, selfhood, or self-identity, the very concept of 'I', is acquired by man through interaction with other men, with whom he com- municates through symbols (see next chapter for detailed dis- cussion). A man is born into a society with a culture and a structure by which he is shaped. This socio-cultural reality is an objective fact which confronts him from the outside. To that extent the group is prior to the individual. This does not mean that man is dwarfed by that reality and that his nature and his will are deter- mined by it. Man also develops an autonomy of his own, his 'self', by which he reacts on society. The relationship between man and society is thus a dialectical one (Radcliffe-Brown 1952:193–4; Berger and Luckman 1967). But we must not exaggerate the extent to which a man is free from the groups to which he belongs. For example, in our society we believe that we are free to choose our partner in marriage, that we marry for love. We certainly do so to a large extent. But, as many studies in contemporary industrial societies have shown, most of us marry our social equals. Anthro- pologists call this class endogamy, or homogamy. Endogamy, as we all know, often serves as a mechanism for maintaining the bound- aries of groups and for keeping their membership exclusive to prevent the encroachment of undesirable outsiders into them. In pre-industrial society, endogamy is formally institutionalised, as in traditional Indian society. In our society it is not formally institutionalised, but is, instead, regulated in a subtle, mostly unconscious way through the operation of a body of symbols that we acquire through socialisation. The status groups to which we belong implant special 'agents' in our personalities and make us respond to certain categories of members of the other sex rather than to other categories (for detailed cases see chapter 6). When we acquire the symbolism implicit in the special 'style of life' of a status group, we in fact thereby automatically acquire the restraints, the collective representations of that group. This means that even when we feel that we are acting as free individuals and following our own individual motives we can in fact be acting as members of groups. Groups act through the action of their members. During an election campaign, candidates, brokers, mediators and voters manipulate one another, following their own private interests. They form factions, action-sets and other alliances. But they at the same time, knowingly or unknowingly, act as members of larger political groups or collectivities.

Some action theory anthropologists tend to take the rules of the game, i.e. the symbols governing social behaviour, as given and as being outside the 'arena' in which the struggle for power takes place, when in fact these symbols are dramatically involved in the whole process at every one of its stages. In other words, this approach assumes stability as it studies change. For an ambitious and clever man to be able to manipulate other men, he must be able to manipulate symbols by interpreting and re-interpreting them.

Early in recent fieldwork in Sierra Leone, I had to make some hurried arrangements, at very short notice, for holding an international academic conference in Freetown. The organisational problems involved seemed to me to be insurmountable. I talked about them informally to a Sierra Leonean friend who was the secretary of a local cultural institute. To my great astonishment the man told me not to worry at all, as he himself would 'fix everything'. At first I thought he was bragging and talking irresponsibly. But within a few days he literally settled all the important matters. Even the most difficult of tasks were magically solved by a short conversation on the telephone with a 'cousin', a 'brother', or a 'friend'. The conference was duly held satisfactorily. What amazed me in particular was that my friend was not a 'leader of men' neither was he an ambitious climber or a schemey 'broker'. He was a very ordinary man, and this increased my admiration. During the following months I began slowly to understand the 'price' that my friend had been paying for such power and influence. 'Cousinhood' in Sierra Leone is a very expensive luxury indeed, both in time and in resources that have to be spent frequently on extensive ceremonials in the course of which the relationships of cousinhood are continuously created and recreated. Some of his 'brothers' turned out to be co-members in the Masonic order and, as I show later (see chapter 6), the cost of such membership in time and money spent on rituals, meetings and banqueting was colossal.

Thus to be able to manipulate others, a man must himself be ready to be manipulated by them. The symbols of 'cousinhood', 'brotherhood' or 'friendship' are collective representations of groupings and only when a man himself participates in these groupings and accepts their values, norms and obligations, only then can he enjoy the privileges of his membership.

If we concentrate exclusively on the study of 'political man' we shall inevitably deal only with his conscious and private endeavour. However, factions, action sets and other 'non-groups' are not 'entities', but partial sections abstracted from a wider and more inclusive social field. No amount of study of egocentric networks will reveal to our view the political structure of society. The egocentric network is meaningful only when it is seen within the context of the 'total network' (Barnes 1968).

Thought structuralists

The other extreme trend in social anthropology at present concentrates on the study of symbols, or of collective representations, often quite out of the context of power relationships. Its orientation is neatly described by Douglas (1968:361): 'Anthropology has moved from the simple analysis of social structures current in the 1940's to the structural analysis of thought systems.'

Anthropologists of this school are influenced in varying degrees by the 'structuralism' of Lévi-Strauss who takes in his stride, among many other variables, both symbolism and power relationships in his analysis. In his study of myth Lévi-Strauss takes it for granted that in any particular context myth is a 'charter for social action'. But, as Leach (1967) points out, he is interested in further problems. He aims at the discovery of the 'language of myth'. He is indeed ultimately concerned with the discovery of nothing less than the 'language', the 'thought structure', behind all culture.

The thought structuralists believe that we see 'objective reality', both natural and social, not as it 'really is', but as 'structured' in terms of logically related thought categories that are built into our psyche. Whatever order there is in nature and in society is largely the outcome of the activities of man under the guidance of his 'programmed' mind. The key to understanding the structure of society is thus, not the analysis of the dynamic on-going patterns of interaction between men, but essentially the 'code', or the logic, the grammar that is explicit in the thought categories and in the systems of relations between them. Thought structuralists are therefore bent on 'breaking the code', for all time and for all culture.

Thought structuralists have greatly refined our understanding of the nature and working of symbols. They have re-emphasised the view – recently weakened by the departure of many anthropologists from some of the tenets of classical Durkheimian sociology – that symbols are not mechanical reflections or epiphenomena, of the political order, but are facts having an autonomy of their own, in their own right. They have drawn attention to some systematic relations existing between different symbols. Like the action theorists in the field of power relations, they have provided anthropology with a number of important concepts and terms that can be used as tools for both analysis and description in the field of symbols.

It is when they lose direct reference to social interaction that they become one-sided and stray from the main stream of social anthropology. Most of them are fully aware of this danger and almost invariably begin their different dissertations with a declaration of faith in 'social structuralism' and a promise to bring their analysis of thought structure to bear upon the dynamic intricacies of social organisation (e.g. Willis 1967). But, as the exposition proceeds, the promised analysis is put off until the end, when it becomes largely inconsequential.

This is in no way an indication of analytical weakness, but is rather a matter of orientation and interest. The problems that this approach poses are not sociological problems, but principally deal with the relations between symbolic categories. Thus, Needham's learned article on Nyoro symbolic classification (1967) deals with a cultural 'puzzle' – that among the Bunyoro, while all that is good and propitious is associated with the *right* hand, the helpful diviner uses his *left* hand in throwing the cowrie shells, which he uses as a divining mechanism. The problem is thus concerned with symbolic categories without much reference to social interaction. Problems of a similar nature are discussed by many others. These are of course very important problems for social anthropology, but only if they are systematically analysed within the context of power relationships.

Symbolic phenomena are highly complex and can be studied from different angles, depending on the theoretical problems posed for analysis. In social anthropology we study the symbolic as it is structured, or systematised, not by a special logic inherent in it, but by the dynamics of interaction between men in society (see Evans-Pritchard 1937). And we study interaction patterns between men as these patterns are constrained, expressed, developed, regulated, or changed by the symbolic. At every stage in the study reference and cross-reference has to be made to both variables.

All this is well known to the thought structuralists, but their dilemma is that too much notice of the involvement of symbols in power relationships will inevitably lead to a departure from the neat logic of thought categories. I believe that this is the source of Beidelman's complaint, twice expressed recently (1968b, 1969), that V. W. Turner 'lacks appreciation of those logical and formal qualities which all symbolic systems . . . possess'. Beidelman himself (1968b:483) points his finger on the real issue when he states that 'Turner emphasizes symbols as expressions of forces; Lévi-Strauss emphasizes their nominal qualities. . .'. The thought structuralists certainly illuminate the formal properties of symbols, but, in the words of Fortes (1967:9) 'at the cost of neutralising the actor'.

Analysis v. description in social science

Most of the practitioners in either of these opposing camps, the action theorists and the thought structuralists, are accomplished anthropologists, with a great deal of work behind them in the 'holistic' study of the interdependence between power relations and symbolic action. Fully aware of the methodological and theoretical implications of what they are doing, they can certainly afford to concentrate on the detailed study of one variable, while bracketing or holding constant the other variable. But it is their disciples who tend to become one-sided and thus lose track of the central problem of the discipline. This is noticeable in some postgraduate work of recent years which has tended to concentrate on one variable to the neglect of the other. The main reason why this one-sidedness appeals to beginners is that it requires little analytical effort. It solves for them the irksome problem of having to find a 'problem' for the analysis of their ethnographical data. To concentrate on the study of either power relationships or symbolism does not involve a great deal of analysis; it poses mainly problems of unidimensional description. An exclusive account of how clever men struggle for power, or of how people behave symbolically, is a categorical description of facts which can be either true or false. It is only by posing problems involving the relations, or the dialectical interdependence, between different variables, that significant analysis can be attempted.

The greatest and most valuable contribution of political anthropology to the study of politics is not so much the typologies of political systems in primitive societies that political anthropologists have developed but the analysis of the symbolism of power relationships generally. The most penetrating part of the now classic 'Introduction' to *African Political Systems* (Fortes and Evans-Pritchard 1940) is not the classification of African traditional politics into the centralised and the decentralised polities, but the analysis of the mystical values associated with political authority. Easton (1959), who argues that 'political anthropology does not yet exist', is right in stating that social anthropologists are interested mainly in non-political institutions like kinship, religion and friendship. What he fails to see, however, is that the specialisation of social anthropology is in the *political interpretation* of these formally non-political institutions. Social anthropologists are interested not in the one-sided effect of politics on these institutions, as he maintains (Easton 1959). On the contrary, they generally seek to explain these non-political institutions in terms of political relations. Thus the analysis of great public symbolic dramas like those of the Tallensi by Fortes (1936; 1945), of the Shilluk by Evans-Pritchard (1948), of the Swazi by Kuper (1947) and Gluckman (1954), of an Arab Shi'ite village by Peters (1963) – to mention only a few – is analysis in political terms. So are studies of fictitious genealogies by

Bohannan (1952) and Peters (1960; 1967), of joking relationships by Colson (1962), and of forms of ancestor worship by Middleton (1960). Even studies of such apparently 'domestic' relationships like marriage by Leach (1961), Peters (1963) and Cohen (1965), and many others are essentially political studies. Gluckman's explanation of the stability of marriage is given in political terms (1950). And Lewis (1971:31) sees spirit possession as a strategy in intersexual politics.

Every monographic study is in effect an experiment in the analysis of the nature of interdependence between these two variables. As in many of the other 'experimental sciences', the greater part of the work of the social anthropologist consists in preparing, or building, 'the experiment'. This consists in analysing and sifting the ethnographic data in order to isolate the two variables from one another and also from those other variables which the anthropologist brackets as 'other things being equal'.

The major difficulty in this procedure is that these variables are not discrete empirical phenomena but analytical isolates, or *aspects* of the same ethnographic facts. Thus, marriage in any society has biological, demographic, domestic, economic, as well as symbolic and political aspects. This is why analysis of field data takes such a long time by anthropologists. It is also the reason why the more analytically advanced an anthropological study is, the more 'over-simplified' its conclusions in the final presentation seem to be. A poorly analysed body of field data presents a confused account, cluttered with a great deal of irrelevant and superficial detail. At best, it gives a 'naturalistic' picture, presenting a mechanical reflection of appearances. An analytical account of the same data on the other hand is like a sketch, showing a few bold lines here and there and weeding out much irrelevant detail (see Lienhardt 1964). The most profound anthropologists have written the clearest and the simplest monographs. Evans-Pritchard is a case in point. This is not simply a matter of genius. 'Genius', as the saying goes, 'is ninety-nine per cent hard work.'

Political man — symbolist man   4

Institutional differentiation and the return to multiplexity

Structural-functionalism required stability of socio-cultural arrangements and a holistic coverage, for technical, not theoretical, considerations. But the requirement that the societies which we study should be institutionally undifferentiated, on the other hand, is a purely theoretical issue. Methodologically, it is indeed much easier to study institutionally differentiated situations than institutionally undifferentiated ones. In institutionally differentiated situations you know the exact location of the realms of economics, politics, religion and the family. In institutionally undifferentiated situations on the other hand you will have to undertake rigorous analysis in order to identify and isolate each realm from the complexity of the socio-cultural mass. For example, in a society like that of the Tallensi (Fortes 1945, 1949) where kinship provides the general idiom articulating economic, jural, political, moral and ritual relations, analysis aims at separating from the general kinship idiom those aspects that are political, those that are economic, and so on. The very competence of social anthropology is this institutional differentiation of institutionally undifferentiated sociocultural situations.

The implications of all this for the study of industrial society are obvious. Social anthropology is concerned with the study of custom (Gluckman 1942, 1965a; Fortes 1953). Custom exists mainly in institutionally undifferentiated, small-scale, societies where relationships tend to be multiplex, each relationship serving different interests. Industrial society on the other hand is institutionally differentiated and is governed not by custom but by contract and relationships tend to be 'single-stranded', each serving one interest. Social anthropological analysis therefore does not apply to its study, which will therefore have to be left to sociology and to other specialised social disciplines.

This is a very well-entrenched view and is based on the theories of the great sociologists of the turn of the present century. It is deeply rooted in the evolutionary formulations of those sociologists who see social change leading in one direction: from 'primitive' society which is dominated by status to modern industrial society which is dominated by contract. From the non-rationality of custom to the rationality of bureaucracy.

The argument here is very weighty and is supported, not only by theoretical assumptions, but also by what is advanced as the 'evidence' of objective reality. The institutions of kinship and religion, which dominated 'primitive' society, have in many places disintegrated under the impact of industrialisation. Some political scientists use the term 'secularisation' to describe the process involved in this assumed evolutionary change. 'Secularisation', write Almond and Powell (1966:24), 'is the process whereby men become increasingly rational, analytical and empirical in their political action.'

Further elaboration of this view has been worked out by a number of anthropologists. An important contribution in this respect is Gluckman's hypothesis about the nature of ritualisation (1963). This states that in 'primitive' society, where relationships are multiplex, ritualisation is intense as it serves as a necessary mechanism for role, and hence institutional, differentiation. In modern society, on the other hand, roles, and hence institutions, tend to be formally differentiated and therefore no need for ritualisation exists.

But I believe that it is time now to re-examine these formulations in the light of recent developments in the study of both simple and industrial societies.

The great sociologists exaggerated the qualitative differences between the nature of primitive society and that of industrial society. This is partly due to the inadequate ethnography available to them. They had to rely on reports of untrained observers of primitive society, who dwelt in their reports on the blind and non-rational nature of custom, which was thought to govern social relationships in that type of society. The anthropologists who came after them managed to collect more authentic data in the field, but in their microsociological zeal have often isolated for their studies, small-scale settlements which in most cases can in no way be described as totalities of social life. Turner's masterly analysis of ritual symbolism among the Ndembu (1957) was carried out in villages with only about thirty inhabitants, including men, women and children. The number of adults of both sexes in such a village must have been less than ten. In such a 'society' if one man sneezes the whole 'social structure' will indeed catch a cold. Turner, however, knowingly chose such a small-scale community, for heuristic considerations, to tackle a specific problem. But other anthropologists sought to analyse the entire politico-cultural order of a society within such a universe.

This can be seen from one particular example, when the anthropologist studying an African tribe looked for the familiar forms of social structure but failed to find any. Social life in the villages that he studied seemed to be chaotic. Nevertheless, the people lived in peace and friendliness. To deal with this seeming paradox, the author undertook the analysis of ingeniously detailed and extensive case studies in order to conclude that the villages achieve order and peace through the very petty disputes which bedevil their life, as in dealing with them they reaffirm their relationships. But from occasional remarks which the author makes in the monograph, an altogether different picture emerges. The reader learns that the villagers are highly individualistic and culturally sophisticated. They are among the first tribal groups in the area to come under the influence of European missionaries, and today they all profess to be

Christians. They began migrating for wage employment several decades ago and today the majority of the men are absent from the villages. They are a 'go-ahead people' enjoying a monopoly of the best jobs in towns, and supplying the African population in those towns with proportionately more leaders than other tribal groups. We also gather from the book that law and order in the villages are maintained by the central administration. Furthermore, land and other natural resources necessary for the subsistence section of the village economy are abundant and their distribution is not controlled by headmen. And because of the attraction of the town, men were no longer interested in the village headmanship. The acquisition of wealth no longer required local co-operation since the main source of wealth now was in the distant towns. It is obvious from all this that the major economic and political relations interlock outside the village. Is it, therefore, at all surprising that the anthropologist should fail to find in the village today the familiar monolithic principles of social organisation which have been reported for the more primitive, subsistence-level, societies? If law and order were maintained by the central government, if a great deal of money came from wage labour in the towns, if there was no scarcity of resources and no competition for positions of power within the village why should the 'traditional structural forms' exist? Indeed if previous analyses in social anthropology are valid, the sociological paradox would have been, not that those forms did not exist, but if they have existed.

Many other studies of small-scale settlements that were carried out during the 1940s and 1950s by anthropologists suffer from the same limitation. This was particularly the case with African studies. One factor which contributed to this limitation is that when anthropologists conducted their studies, those settlements had been under colonial rule. In British West Africa, 'indirect rule' provided an umbrella for the artificial preservation, indeed sometimes for the creation, of local, small-scale 'tribal' groups, even though at about the same time fundamental changes in scale, both economic and political, were drawing the members of those groups into the arenas of national-level, contractual, relationships of various sorts. Indeed, as we are now beginning to discover more and more of the facts about pre-colonial days in Africa, we begin to realise that the ideal model of the small-scale isolated primitive community is a myth. Nearly everywhere in Africa there were continual movements and contacts between localities, peoples, and whole regions. In West Africa, the outlines of about a thousand years of pre-colonial history tell the story of the rise and fall of states and empires, of large-scale economic, political and cultural contacts with the powers and centres of civilisation in the Mediterranean.

In a similar way, the great sociologists, and the sociologists who have followed in their footsteps, have tended to emphasise the rational and the contractual and to minimise the significance of the symbolic in the structure of modern industrial society. This is perhaps a harsh statement, for there are certainly sociologists who have studied the development and functioning of norms, values, symbols and ideology in contemporary society and indeed some important work has been produced in this field.

But there are two main points that arise here about the relative importance of these studies at present. First, while it is true that sociology has tackled almost every field in social life – some would even include social anthropology within its domain – there has been an unmistakable trend in the last two or three decades in the important centres of sociology on both sides of the Atlantic towards the concentration on narrow and fragmentary empirical studies, particularly of quantifiable phenomena. Even a casual look at the current numbers of the *American Sociological Review* and *Sociology*, which are platforms for the main body of American and British sociology, the strong concentration on problems that lend themselves to rigorous quantification and sophisticated statistical treatment become apparent. This is accompanied by a new emphasis on methodology which in some cases is again becoming an end in itself rather than as a means to an end. The point is that there are many kinds of symbolic phenomena that are simply not amenable to this kind of treatment, unless they are mutilated beyond recognition. This is because symbolic behaviour is dramatic behaviour and its analysis cannot be effected through the computer. The computer can certainly be employed to great advantage in measuring such variables as age, sex, occupation, length of residence in a place, birthplace, and even attendance at ceremonies and time spent on these, and there is an increasing number of anthropologists who are making use of it for such purposes. But the analysis of the political significance of a specific ideology, of a public ceremonial, or of a religious drama, cannot – at least at the present state of our knowledge – be done quantitatively. There are certainly great possibilities of quantification in this field in such a large-scale project as that of the Human Relations Files, which make it possible to establish correlations between cultural variables as reported for several hundreds of societies. But such an effort is still at its infancy. One result of all this is that 'scientifically inclined' sociologists tend to concentrate on the study of quantifiable phenomena and to avoid those phenomena that are difficult to quantify.

Second, even when contemporary social scientists choose to deal with symbolic behaviour, they tend to operate with a mechanical conception of socio-cultural causation, rather than with a dialectical one. The functions of this kind of behaviour are thus seen as being intended by individuals and groups, and are mostly formal functions. This approach is particularly evident in social psychology. In my view, even Goffman's analysis in his *The Presentation of Self in Everyday Life* (1969) suffers from the same limitation, despite the fact that the author himself states that he is dealing with both intended and unintended patterns of action. The functions of symbolic behaviour are almost by definition unintended by the actors. When men in an African Muslim polity gather in a congregation to pray on Friday, they do not say: Let us pray in order to consolidate the weakening position of the chief, or to enhance the moral distinctiveness of the community. They are mostly unaware of these functions, their motives in performing the prayer being mixed and varied, often having nothing to do directly with politicking.

The dichotomous formulations of the great sociologists overlook the subtleties of the process of institutionalisation and symbolisation. A usage or practice or norm becomes institutionalised only when it becomes accommodated within the institutional structure of society (Wiese and Becker 1952). A political order becomes institutionalised in a society when it becomes integrated within its economic, religious, moral and ideological structure. Indeed it is only in this way that it becomes validated. Thus, the process of institutional differentiation which accompanies change from a primitive to an industrial society is counterbalanced by the process of institutional reintegration, though on a different level. On the individual level, single-stranded relationships soon tend to become multiplex relationships again. Homans (1951:131–55) explains this in terms of a 'social surplus' theory, maintaining that whenever men come together within the framework of a formal single-interest association, they

53

interact as whole personalities and soon create informal social relationships which are not necessary parts of the formal association.

The politico-symbolic dimensions of selfhood

This aspect of the process of institutionalisation will be better understood if we probe into the socio-symbolic aspects of selfhood. It is true that there is a great deal of institutional differentiation in contemporary industrial society, but the different, formally delineated, institutions are lived by total personalities – by 'selves'. A person plays different roles and enters into contractual single-stranded relationships with different persons. Thus, an employee is involved within the firm in which he works by virtue of only his role as worker. Similarly, when he joins a formal political association he is formally involved by virtue of only that role. It is thus possible to analyse the self in terms of separate roles, each played in a separate social sphere. Psychologists describe this as 'segmental involvement', i.e. that the person is involved in these single-stranded organisations by virtue of only a segment of his personality. The collectivity of roles that a person plays in society have been called by Radcliffe-Brown (1952:188–204) the 'social personality'.

But the personality can be segmented in this way only to a limited degree, as otherwise the person will not be able to perform his specialised roles as a human being. It is true that the worker is involved in his job by virtue of only one contractual role. But that role can be played effectively only if the worker brought into it the whole of his personality. If this is not so, i.e. if the role is purely mechanical and does not need any spontaneous human judgment, then it will be depersonalised and hence made redundant as a human role. It will be replaceable by a machine. Thus no matter how specialised a contractual role is, it requires the judgment and the action of the total person and involves, at least at some stages, interaction with other human beings. This means that even for the performance of a specialised contractual role the total personality becomes involved. Some roles require more involvement of the total person than others.

Thus a person cannot operate in society unless he acts as *one* self. This oneness, or selfhood, can be achieved only when the various roles that a person plays are integrated together within one unified system or whole – the 'I' or 'Ego'. If the roles are incompatible, as they indeed often tend to be, they will have to be reconciled with one another through some mediating mechanisms.

This psychic system, or selfhood, is not something which we acquire by birth, by virtue of our being human. It is achieved through social interaction with other men. What is more, it is not achieved once and for all during our early childhood, as some psychoanalysts maintain, but is perpetually in the making. Our selfhood is continually faced with disintegration by the subversive changes which characterise our involvement in social roles and activities. Our identity is not a purely subjective construction. The subjective self is precarious and can be maintained only through continuous interaction in society.

This problem of the continuous development and maintenance of selfhood becomes more acute, the more the roles that we play in society are fragmentary and incompatible with one another. We can thus postulate a state of balance, or equilibrium, between the fragmentary nature of social roles and the strength of selfhood. The more the fragmentation and the incompatibility of our roles in society, the greater the strength of selfhood. When a man fails to achieve such an equilibrium in his own personality, he will lose his selfhood, the oneness of the 'I', and thus become a 'psychic case', in need of clinical treatment.

Selfhood is achieved by man when he interacts with other men with the totality of his personality. In the performance of a single, highly-specialised, contractual role, the totality of the self is least involved. On the other hand, maximum involvement of the self is achieved through non-contractual, non-utilitarian roles and activities in symbolic action. As Morris (1972:84) puts it: 'People are at their most individual and personal when they engage in drama.'

Symbolic action is almost by definition action involving the totality of the person, including his cognition, feeling and sensation. This is a point greatly illuminated by Turner's analysis of the ritual symbol (1964). The ritual symbol condenses in one formation a multiplicity of discrepant meanings as well as a polarity of sensorial and ideological features. As symbols vary in their potency, the more potent the symbol the more total the involvement of the self.

In nearly all social action, both the symbolic and the contractual are present, but some activities are more symbolic and less contractual than others. At the one end there are ideally conceived

POLITICAL MAN—SYMBOLIST MAN

purely contractual, segmental roles, while at the other end there are purely symbolic patterns of action involving only the totality of the person. Turner (1969) has recently illuminated this distinction, referring to the one extreme end of the continuum as 'structure', and to the other end as 'communitas'. Most social activities are partly symbolic and partly contractual.

Thus, in the symbolic act, the different, often disparate, roles are integrated together, within the unity of selfhood. If the opportunity for symbolic action is minimal in our ordinary involvement in 'structure' – to use Turner's terms – if our job involves intense, sometimes incompatible contractual activities, without the opportunity for a sufficient measure of symbolic action, we seek to redress the balance by engaging in recreational activities. Often we need a periodical leave from our job not because we are physically exhausted, but because the contractual 'structure', in which we are caught up in our ordinary daily life, is increasingly and accumulatively undermining the totality of our selfhood. We often need the periodical leave, not to be alone with ourself, but, on the contrary, to be in 'communitas' with others, to interact with other people with whom we are least involved contractually.

I believe that it is in this light that we should view Fortes's contention and prolonged polemic to the effect that even if we take away the economico-political interests from kinship relationships, there will still be an irreducible element left (see Fortes 1949). The source of obligation, of the 'ought', behind this irreducible element is the process of the continual creation and recreation of selfhood. There can be no idea of the self without symbolic interaction with others. This is axiomatic. But of course symbolic interaction is not confined to kinship or friendship but is an element in nearly all social relationships.

The discussion here is verging on psychology. Indeed the charge of psychologism, of the attempt to explain socio-cultural phenomena in terms of psychic processes and psychic needs, has always loomed threateningly large whenever social anthropologists took notice of the central focus of all socio-cultural phenomena – man himself. Gluckman, who has discussed at length the relation between social conflict and ritual, has been vexed for years by those critics, particularly from the USA, who thought that his explanation of social conflict was given in terms of psychic conflict. For a social anthropologist developing within the structural-functionalist tradition, there is nothing more annoying. In reply to those critics, Gluckman has conducted a continual polemic to point out that, although psychic conflict can be a concomitant of social conflict, his explanation is purely sociological and has nothing to do with psychology. Rituals of rebellions are not the continual, spontaneous creations of men experiencing social conflict, but are social facts in their own right, the collective representations that constrain the individual and that are handed down from generation to generation. Individuals performing them might have been suffering psychic conflict, which may be mitigated by the ritual. But, on the other hand, many other men who did not suffer such conflicts were induced by the rituals to experience the conflicts. Psychic conflict is brought about by the social order and it is the ongoing social order which provides the social mechanisms for the repetitive, temporary, resolution of these conflicts.

This argument will of course in turn be open to the charge, often made against social anthropology generally, that it eliminates man, by taking him to be shaped deterministically by exterior forces, leaving nothing to individual creativity and freedom of the will.

The main reason for the rise of this controversy is that many social anthropologists, true to their synchronic and holistic approach, have studied societies as stable, ongoing systems of relations. Turner and Gluckman have assumed the systems which they analysed to be in a state of equilibrium, or of repetitive equilibria. In such a system both conflict and the rituals resolving it are given by the system. Under these circumstances, selfhood can be regarded as a constant, not a variable, and can therefore either be kept out of the analysis, or can be only 'naïvely' conceived and assumed, leaving its detailed study to the competence of the psychologist or psychoanalyst (see Devons and Gluckman 1964).

But if the heuristic assumption of 'stability' is abandoned for a more dynamic view; if we study changing systems of variables, not systems in equilibria, if we study the symbolisation processes, the processes of institutionalisation, then the perennial problem of selfhood will become a significant variable in socio-cultural processes. The creativity and inventiveness of man will become a factor directly involved in socio-cultural change.

It is true that at any one time the patterns of symbolic activity which ensure the maintenance of our selfhood are given by the society. When society changes, men tend for some time to continue, indeed to struggle hard to preserve their identity, their selfhood, in the old traditional ways. Social change is in a way always a threat to our selfhood, particularly if it involves changes in roles. We tenaciously try to maintain our selfhood by giving new interpretation to our patterns of symbolic action. In the short run, a rapid change in the structure of selfhood is tantamount to self-negation and to psychological suicide. We can fairly easily change our formal economic and political behaviour. Economic-political behaviour is governed by contractual, rationally thought out considerations and for a long time we try to convince ourselves that this change is accidental, is part of our life history and need not affect our 'culture', our patterns of kinship and friendship, the patterns of our interaction with men in general. Whenever possible, we try to adjust to the new politico-economic structure by reinterpreting our existing patterns of symbolic behaviour. We try to maintain our traditional patterns of kinship and friendship by adapting them in such a way as to serve as many of the new purposes as possible. This is why socio-cultural change proceeds dialectically, not mechanically. Selfhood is not a mechanical reflection of power relations, but is an autonomous entity, a system in its own right, which can react on the power order and modify it. A change in the power order does not automatically bring about a change in the structure of selfhood.

The battle for the maintenance of selfhood in the face of the continuous subversive processes operating in society is one of the perennial problems of man. It arises in both simple and modern society. It tends to be more acute in modern society because of the tendency of contractual roles to be more fragmentary, dispersed and incompatible. These subversive processes become a serious threat when rapid structural change takes place, when men go through stress. The equilibrium between selfhood and the disparate roles is seriously disturbed. As a result, there is an active search for a new equilibrium, for a modified symbolic order to accommodate the self within the new alignments of power.

Here the creativity of man begins to operate. When we exhaust the possibilities of the traditional patterns of symbolic behaviour which maintain our identity in the new situation, we try subjectively to invent new symbolic patterns of our own to deal with the new patterns of interaction. But subjective selfhood is a precarious entity. Our inner imagination and thought are unstable and uncertain. Our ideas and symbolic formations are vague and lacking in objectivity because they are not shared with others.

But men seldom face this continuing battle of selfhood entirely unassisted. This assistance can take different forms which may operate simultaneously. As men in distress talk about their problems and their anxieties they also pool down their experiences and their symbolic formulations. Some individuals may prove to be more perceptive, more creative, and more articulate than others, and their formulations may appeal more than those of others to a wide collectivity of people who are in the throes of the same problem. These are the charismatic leaders who objectify new relationships and give definite symbolic forms to vaguely experienced subjective ideas and images. Once formulated, these symbolic constructions become an objective reality confronting the individual from the outside. They are no longer the spontaneous creation of men experiencing distress (see Berger and Luckman 1967). In the process, these symbolic forms become simplified, as they shed the irrelevant details created by the circumstances of time and space and as their central theme is dramatised. They become routinised through the introduction of patterns of repetition.

These processes, however, do not occur in a socio-cultural vacuum but are intimately interrelated with other processes within a political context consisting of competing and quarrelling groups. The new symbolic formulations are greatly conditioned by this political context. What is more, existing political groups, the large corporations in our industrial society, are always locked in a struggle with one another over capturing not a segment of the personalities of their members, but as much of the total self of the members as possible. A monolithic political party will try to absorb the thinking, feeling and action of its members. Subsidiary organisations are developed to cater for the youth of the members to ensure their early socialisation in the ideology of the party. Clubs, societies, associations, funds, entertainment, schools and a host of other organisational frames are provided. Similarly, a big industrial corporation will cater for the entire well-being of the workers, providing them with entertainment, refreshment, schemes for aid and so on. The members of the group are persuaded, not only to try and promote the general aims of the corporation, but also to develop comradeship with one another, to eat, drink, play and pray together. This is not necessarily because the total involvement of the members in the corporation is necessary for the functioning of the corporation, but also to inhibit other, rival corporations from capturing the totality of the selves of their members.

The totality of the self is thus subject to a most intensive competition between various types of power groups. Every major interest group tries to offer its members a totality of scheme for life, a solution of the problems of man in contemporary society. Every major interest group tries to present its members with a ready-made blue-print for living, with a design for selfhood. A group organised rationally and bureaucratically which operates as part of the legal structure of society will need little of the totality of man, provided that no rival group will try to claim it. But when these conditions do not exist, when the group is illegal, when it is not rationally organised, then it will operate by means of categorical obligations rather than of contract. Its hold on its members will be normative and will thus involve their total selves, not specialised segmental roles.

The politicisation of the
perennial problems of human existence

The threat to selfhood comes not only from the contradictory roles within the self, but also from the perpetual threats of anomie and marginality posed by the unresolved problems of human existence in the universe: the meaning of life and death, fortune and misfortune, good and evil, health and sickness, growth and decay. It is true that with industrialisation there is an increasing tendency towards rationalisation in thinking and in social organisation. This goes together with the advance of science and technology. As a result, the realm of the mystical in different areas of social life is pushed back. The secrets of many diseases, the planets, biological inheritance, conception, fertility of the soil, and other problems which in simple society are explained in mystical terms are unravelled and explained by science.

But there are other problems in life which science has never and perhaps will never solve rationally. Talk to a 'primitive' man about interplanetary travel or about chemical processes, and you will immediately see that he is many centuries behind you in his knowledge. But talk with him about the meaning of life and death, fortune and misfortune, the nature of political authority, the various crises in the life of the individual, and you will immediately discover that you are in fact talking to a contemporary. These problems have had no final solutions, and they continue to challenge our thinking and feeling. In the Jewish burial ceremony – as in that of many other religious traditions – the cantor dramatically poses the central problem of human existence, when he addresses the dead before the grave is sealed: 'From where did you come, and where are you going?'

These are not trivial questions but are for men everywhere, at least at some stages in their lives, more fundamental than many of the problems posed and resolved by science. Indeed, unless some adequate 'solutions' for them were provided, social order would suffer greatly. If the enigma of death, for example, is not 'explained' and resolved somehow, if men realise deeply that they are doomed to oblivion, if they know that their beloved ones are gone for good, if they live under the constant shadow of death, their fear and grief will paralyse their thinking and acting and they will not be able to live a 'normal' life.

Modern man, not less than primitive man, needs a solution to these problems. These solutions are always symbolic constructions. They are only partly rational. Many religious traditions maintain that when we depart from this life, we continue to exist in another realm. In Freetown, Sierra Leone, the highly educated and anglicised Creoles, including university professors who have distinguished themselves in the 'exact sciences', maintain that their dead relatives continue to live as spirits around them. They address them, reason with them, try to 'keep them happy', offering them food and libations of water and alcohol and communicating with them through the manipulation of kolanuts and through dreams. The Creoles see no contradiction between this and their Christian beliefs. They say that the spirits of the dead are part of the 'communion of saints'. There is nothing illogical or 'unscientific' about this as long as the eternal question 'From where did you come and where are you going?' remains unsolved. Fundamentally, no solution of this problem is 'more scientific' than another solution.

In many western industrial societies formally organised religion has been dwindling, though as mentioned earlier, a number of studies indicate revival in other societies. Wilson writes (1969:22) that average Sunday attendance in church is less than 3 per cent in Norway and between 10 and 15 per cent in England. But, he points out, the demand on religion for rites of passage continues with little change. The three most crucial rites of passage, birth, marriage and death, are still administered by the established religion. In Britain only about 30 per cent of marriages are conducted in registry offices, while the remaining 70 per cent are solemnised by religion. The proportion is much higher in the case of burial, where religious officiation is a matter of routine.

Similarly, men seek explanations for the singularity of misfortune, of why we, not others, should have this or that accident, this or that occurrence of bad luck; explanations that are more informative and more comforting than the negative 'no-explanations' of chance. We are no less preoccupied with this problem than the 'primitive' Azande (Evans-Pritchard 1937) and our explanations are no more rational.

Here, as with the question of selfhood, we do not face these problems of human existence on our own. For most of us, the major groups, the great corporations, to which we belong take care of this side of our life as well as of other sides. They provide us with explanations, sharpened by the endeavours of expert ideologists, and also offer remedies. They teach us that we die, but continue to live within our lineage, motherland, nation, the party. We are made to identify with and project ourselves into a continuing, eternal, force which is larger than ourselves, within which we should continue to live after our death. This is developed, objectified, and inculcated in ceremonies of all sorts: state funerals, cenotaphs, memorial services. Our misfortunes, we are told, are due to the evil machinations of our enemies: Imperialism, World Communism, Zionism and others.

The perennial problems of man are thus fundamental issues which, under certain structural circumstances, are often seized upon by interest groups to achieve their organisational functions and realise their ends. Groups that can organise their activities formally and legally for the pursuit of their aims need make little use of these issues. The allegiance of their members is ensured through contractual mechanisms. But when for some reason a group has to organise informally, then contractual mechanisms give way to obligation. Compliance is achieved through categorical imperatives which impel the total man to act in conformity with the aims of the group. To achieve this, the strong emotional anxieties of men in facing the problems of existence are heightened, developed, given expression and channelled into action in the interests of the group. Thus, in the UK, for example, where formal organisation is part of a long-standing liberal tradition, the horrifying prospects of death are minimal. Funerals are small, and mourning brief. We push death out of our thinking and try to keep ourselves too happy and occupied to be reminded of it. We are aided in this by the improved medical services, prolongation of life, and pain-killing drugs. When the hour finally comes, many of us turn to organised religion for some comfort to alleviate the pangs of death and to conduct us on our last journey to 'the other world'.

In all these matters, a scientist is not much more rational in his thinking than a 'primitive' man. Some of the most eminent scientists of our time explain these problems in terms of the will and schemes of God. And if this is the case with scientists who are relatively a small minority, it is far more so in the case of ordinary people who are the bulk of the society. We cannot maintain our selfhood and poise in a completely unknown world. In place of the unknowable we substitute belief in a symbolically constructed universe in which we can feel reasonably at home.

In both the problem of selfhood and that of human existence, the different groups to which we belong provide solutions from their own standpoints. Many of us accept ready-made symbolic mechanisms aimed at resolving these problems. We are often helped by 'specialists' who guide our uncertain thoughts and provide us with objective symbols which 'express the inexpressible' under which we can conduct our life.

However, because of the dynamic nature of modern industrial society, of the continuous change in technology, of the rise and fall of interest groups of all sorts, our ideologies and hence our selfhood and our place in the universe are continually challenged.

But we are always active in accommodating our symbolic world to the new realities. We continuously create new syntheses, new symbolic patterns to overcome our difficulties. Some of us may prove more creative in this respect than others. Here, too, as individual 'artists' or 'ideologists' create new symbolic formations to deal with the current problems of men, the great corporations seize upon them by 'promoting' them or simply 'buying' them, to utilise them for their own ends. In time, the creative symbolic synthesis loses its moral or obligatory nature. It ceases to involve the total personality and becomes part of a segmental role. The obligatory becomes contractual. The 'holistic' becomes 'partisan'. It is because of this tendency in modern industrial society that Marcuse (1964) describes modern man as being 'one-dimensional man'. But this is to lose faith in the unceasing creativity of man. This creativity can not be crushed by the great corporations. Even under the most absolute totalitarianism in contemporary industrial society this creativity has been at work.

The symbols governing the interaction that develop our selfhood, as well as those dealing with the perennial problems of human existence, are highly autonomous. They are never the mechanical reflections of power relationships. They have an existence of their own. Amidst change in the relationships of power, they display a great deal of continuity. When one symbolic form becomes incompatible with the new situation, another is developed to fulfil the same function.

The problems of selfhood and of human existence are fundamental forces behind a wide variety of symbolic forms. They are two main sources of obligation, of 'oughts', of the categorical imperatives that operate in society. They are not innate in biological man, but are conditioned, if not created, by society. They are behind two forms of symbolic complexes. The one governing interaction between one man and another. The other governing our relation with the universe. In simple society, the one is manifested mainly in kinship, while the other mainly in ritual. But, as I have argued earlier, these two forms, though distinct in a number of ways, are highly interconnected and interchangeable in their social functions. When in a social system one is particularly weak, the other is exploited to fill in the gap.

Those two sources of obligation are everywhere, in both primitive and industrial societies, exploited in articulating the organisational functions of political groups. Even the most formal of groups in contemporary society have to supplement contractual relationships with symbolic, normative ones in their organisation. The less formal the group, the more the exploitation of symbolic patterns of action in it. Where contract fails, moral or ritual obligations are put into use. And this leads the discussion to an examination of the dynamics of group organisation.

Symbolic strategies in group organisation

5

In industrial society, no less than in primitive society, there are wide ranges of organisational functions, on almost all levels of political organisation, that are effected not through rationally planned arrangements, but through non-rational symbolic formations and activities. This becomes clear from the analysis of the organisation of interest groups.

Societies consist of a multiplicity of interest groupings, of all sizes and sorts, that quarrel, compete, federate, cross-cut, and overlap with one another, to protect or increase their share of power. These are thus essentially political groupings and their activities determine the distribution, maintenance and exercise of power in society. These groups operate by means of their organisation. A collectivity of people without organisation is not a group. It is only to the extent that the collectivity has mechanisms for the direct or indirect co-ordination of action that it becomes a political group. I think we shall only stultify the analysis if we add to the sociological characteristics of a group, that its members should know, and interact face to face with one another or that they should be aware of their own grouping or of their membership in the group. Through our style of life and social activities, we may develop the interests of a 'class' or status group without even realising that we are in fact doing so or that we are at all 'members' in such groups. There are indeed many groups that are in this sense 'invisible' and it is part of the task of the sociology of politics to 'discover', identify, and analyse the structure of these groups.

This focus on interest groups does not imply the assumption that these groups exhaust the whole universe of social organisation. It does not in any way belittle the importance of the study of the biographies and private networks of individuals who are involved in the multiplicity and complexity of these interest groups. Neither does it deny the existence of what some anthropologists have so disarmingly labelled as 'non-groups'. Social life is so varied and complex that one can legitimately isolate any social phenomenon on any level, for detailed analysis. The question is not which isolate, or what level, is more valid to study than which, but which is helpful in tackling a particular problem, leading to further analysis and generating new hypotheses. Within the structure of the modern state it is interest groups that constitute the 'bony structure of power' or what sociologists call 'social stratification'.

Political groups differ in the significance of the interests which they articulate, and hence in the degree of the involvement of the personalities of their members in them. Some groups are more fundamental to a person than other groups.

The organisation of a group consists in the development and maintenance of mechanisms, or patterns of activities, that are aimed at the solution of a number of basic operational problems: the problem of distinctiveness, of communication, decision-making, authority, ideology and discipline.

A group is formally organised when these functions are arranged rationally on bureaucratic lines and its aims are specifically known. As Weber shows, this kind of organisation, or association, is the most efficient type of human organisation, and in industrial societies most groups attempt to make use of it.

Informal organisation

But even in the advanced liberal industrial societies there are some structural conditions under which some interest groups cannot organise themselves on formal lines. Their formal organisation may be opposed by the state or by other groups within the state, or may be generally incompatible with the basic principles of the society. The Creoles (who are discussed in the next chapter) are only 1.9 per cent of the population of Sierra Leone, yet they dominate the civil service and the professions in the whole country. They have been under strong pressure since independence and have attempted to co-ordinate their political action by means of a Creole political party. But they soon discovered that it would be fatal for their position to do so because the political system in the country is based on the principle of 'one man one vote' which means that eventually their privilege and power would be cut down to size. They therefore began to talk against 'tribalism' and to declare themselves to be Sierra Leoneans. At the same time they resorted to co-ordinating their political action by manipulating different symbolic activities that ostensibly had nothing to do with politics (for more details see chapter 6; also Cohen 1971). In many other African countries, interest groups that after independence could not continue to be organised on formal lines began to articulate their organisation in terms of ethnicity. Again, in the industrial societies of the West, because of the underlying formal principles of egalitarianism, privileged classes cannot organise formally as classes. For example, as is shown in the next chapter, élites co-operate with one another in ways that are incompatible with their formal position in society and cannot therefore organise this co-operation in a formal way. They therefore resort to informal organisational mechanisms.

There are other structural conditions under which interest groups cannot organise formally. In some cases the interests they represent may be newly developed and are not yet articulated in terms of an organisation which is accommodated within the formal structure of the society. Or, the members of the group may be too poor or too ignorant to go through the usually highly complicated and costly legal and bureaucratic formalities required for the establishment of a formal association. Or, a combination of these circumstances may occur.

Under these conditions the organisation of the group is articulated on informal lines, making use of the kinship, friendship, ritual, ceremonial and other forms of symbolic patterns and activities that are implicit in what is known as 'style of life'.

This strategy of organising a group on the basis of different types of obligation which are not consciously adopted or planned, is likely to be wasteful in time and energy, and is not as efficient in achieving the group's ends as formal organisation. For example, instead of organising an official meeting for the members of the group to discuss a current problem, the informal group will attend a ceremonial during which the problem is only informally and unsystematically discussed, amidst a great deal of what for the achievement of the ends of the group are irrelevant symbolic activities, though these activities may at the same time satisfy some important personality needs.

The difference between formal and informal group organisation here is a matter of degree. Nearly all formally organised groups need symbolic patterns of behaviour at certain points, or at certain periods, in their organisation. What is more, the members of a formal group soon develop informal patterns of interaction which have nothing to do with the formal structure of the group but which, nevertheless, become part of the total organisation and functioning of the group. Informal groups on the other hand tend to have some contractual elements or aspects at different points in their structure. Political groups can thus be ranged on one organisational continuum with the most formal at the one end and the most informal at the other.

The organisation of a group can be conceived as having two dimensions, the contractual and the normative, or the formal and the informal. A great deal of light has been thrown on the nature of formal organisation by sociologists and there is extensive literature dealing with it. It is mainly with group organisations at the other end of the continuum, i.e. those whose organisation is predominantly informal, that I am particularly dealing here. These informal groupings pervade the whole formal structure of contemporary industrial society and their analysis is of central importance for all students of society.

Organisational functions

The organisation of a group consists in the development and maintenance of mechanisms that provide solutions to a number of organisational problems.

I DISTINCTIVENESS (OR BOUNDARIES)

To operate effectively, a group must define its membership and its sphere of operation, by defining its identity and its exclusiveness, within the political field in which it operates. The more privileged the group, the more will it try to prevent men from inferior groups from infiltrating into its ranks. An underprivileged group on the other hand may have to define its membership because it is only by organising itself that it can struggle effectively with other groups over larger shares of power.

As demonstrated in the next chapter, informal groups adopt one or more of a number of symbolic forms to define their distinctiveness.

Mythologies of descent

A group can articulate its distinctiveness in terms of a principle of unilineal descent, claiming that the members of the group have descended from a common ancestor. Generally speaking, descent can be traced patrilineally, through males, or matrilineally, through females, or double unilineally, through both. The relationships between the different members within the group are articulated in terms of a genealogy. As anthropologists have demonstrated in the analysis of numerous cases from illiterate societies, a genealogy of this type is a charter for action, not an historical document. Its symbols are continuously manipulated in order to adjust it to changing demographic, political and economic conditions (see Bohannan 1952; Peters 1960).

A principle of descent is usually supported by such genetic 'theories' as that blood is inherited in a certain line, that the whole lineage has 'one blood' or that the members are from one 'womb', 'sinew', or 'stock'. In many simple societies the principle of descent is also supported by cults of the ancestors, associated with beliefs in the mystical powers of those ancestors who can interfere and affect the lives of the living. In many cases, beliefs and practices around totems and taboos work in the same way to bestow distinctiveness on the group.

69

The symbolism of descent has been particularly evident in the articulation of the organisation of small groups. But it is not unknown in the literature of ethnography that large collectivities of populations like the Bedouin of Cyrenaica (Evans-Pritchard 1949; Peters 1960) express their relationships and organisation in terms of a single genealogy.

Although the symbolism of descent allows a good deal of flexibility and manipulation in response to changing realities, a strict form of descent principle is relatively too rigid and too limited to articulate the organisation of large, highly differentiated groupings in rapidly changing societies. Its development and maintenance require relatively long processes associated with generational developments and with patterns of marital and residential stability. It also requires time to allow for the processes of selective forgetting to do their part and is therefore particularly vulnerable to the introduction of literacy and hence of written documents.

Nevertheless, anthropologists have found many cases of its adaptation to contemporary changing conditions. In many developing countries descent groups are adjusting to the new economic and political realities and assuming new functions within the context of the contemporary situation. Cases are known in detail of lineages developing economic enterprises of their own (see, for example, Hill 1963). In other situations, lineages have become political groupings contesting elections corporately as in Arab villages in Israel (see Cohen 1965). In even highly developed countries in America and Europe there are many known cases of large-scale 'family businesses'. In both developing and developed countries mythologies of descent have also been used to validate claims to specialised roles or to high status. Thus in the Arab Middle East there are large numbers of lineages of ritual specialists who claim descent from specific relatives and companions of the Prophet Muhammad, with each lineage keeping a written genealogical 'tree' connecting the living through scores of links with the original ancestors.

In a number of societies there are learned genealogical 'specialists' who, for an appropriate fee, would help you to 'discover' your genealogy. Specialists like these can be found in even the most developed industrial societies. Thus, during the summer months in the UK, notices appear in *The Times*, advertising the services of genealogists who apparently cater for American tourists. In the

American status system a great deal of prestige is attached to English origin (see Packard 1961). Families eager to develop and consolidate a high social status try to support and validate their prestige by 'proving' their claims in the form of a genealogy connecting them with known names in the UK. Often, what matters is not a specific genealogical link, but just a proof of descent from an English 'stock'.

Cults of strict unilineal descent may not be common in contemporary industrial society, but a looser principle is used in almost all societies. Often exclusive groupings like status, 'class', religious or ethnic groups, maintain the claim of being descendants of the same ancestors, though without keeping any specific validating genealogies. These groups tend to be highly endogamous and their members can thus claim to be from the same stock. Meyer Fortes (1959) refers to this as 'bilateral descent'. It is a myth often used in combination with other symbolic mechanisms in order to enhance the identity and exclusiveness of such groups. This myth is exploited by nearly all the groups in the cases discussed in the next chapter.

Alliance under female symbolism
Closely related to descent as mechanisms for achieving distinctiveness are the rules of marriage observed by groups. As Lévi-Strauss (1968:50–1) puts it: 'In human society, kinship is allowed to establish and perpetuate itself only through specific forms of marriage'. The pattern of marriage is everywhere involved in the distribution and maintenance of power between groups. Through the mechanisms of incest and exogamy that operate in all social systems, men are forced to give their sisters and daughters to other men and, in exchange, acquire for themselves the sisters and daughters of other men. The complexity of values associated with women make the female almost everywhere into one of the most potent symbols which is employed in a variety of ways in the struggle for and maintenance of power between groups and individuals.

In many cultures marriage is made to serve as a mechanism for establishing friendship and alliances between men. A collectivity of men can achieve distinctiveness as a group through the practice of endogamy, i.e. marrying in, without intermarrying with other groups. When a principle of strict unilineal descent cannot be adopted by a group, the practice of endogamy can be developed as a substitute in maintaining the distinctiveness of the group. The identity and exclusiveness of the rising generation will be defined both patrilaterally and matrilaterally.

The exchange of women in marriage in or between groups is closely interconnected with the system of the distribution of power between them. The distribution of power in a society is always associated with the institutionalisation of special patterns of marriage, specifying the way women are moved in marriage in and between groups. The regulation of sex and marriage is a fundamental pillar in the politics of racialism in South Africa, Rhodesia and the south of the USA (see Keatley 1963:244–71; Hernton 1969).

There *are* Romeos and Juliets, couples who associate and marry across the lines of class, race, religious, or political cleavages all the time. But these are the exceptions and are often made to strengthen the norms. Sociological studies show these marriages to be highly unstable, as compared with the more 'normal' marriages within the same group (see Gordon 1964). Tension is a concomitant feature in the husband-wife relationship in all societies. But when the couple are from the same interest group there is usually pressure on them to minimise the tension and to preserve the marriage. On the other hand, when the couple are from disparate groups, political forces from one side or both sides will seize on the tension, exaggerate it, widen it, and attempt to break the marriage.

Marriage is everywhere intimately interconnected with social hierarchy. In many stratified societies *homogamy*, i.e. marriage between equals, is combined with *hypergamy*, i.e. the movement of women in marriage from lower to upper strata. In such societies a status group will establish its claim to superiority over another group by refusing to give its women in marriage to men from another group. In many parts of the Arab world status differentiation between groups depends to a large extent on which group give, or do not give, women in marriage to which group. A group can thus achieve distinctiveness through the direct or indirect control of the movement of its women in marriage. (For a more detailed discussion, see cases on pp. 110-18 below. See also Cohen 1970 and 1972.)

Ritual beliefs and practices
Many interest groups achieve distinctiveness by the manipulation of ritual beliefs and practices. A group may maintain a belief in

being 'the chosen people', or in being 'twice born', or may be the bearers of a purer brand of an established cult, or the protégés of a specific saint, or the followers of a special ritual master, or the bearers or guardians of exclusive secret ritual formulae. Beliefs such as these are maintained and kept alive by a variety of ritual activities, including the observance of totems and taboos. The beliefs and the rituals associated with them are standardised and routinised. Often, they become organised in an exclusive organisation. The organisation may even become bureaucratically and formally organised with the formally declared aim of maintaining or promoting the cult.

A group may develop its own exclusive cult or it may adopt the symbolism and organisation of another cult. The possibilities of developing exclusive sects, denominations, congregations, etc., within universal religions are almost limitless – and interest groups have been doing this at all times and in all societies. The extensive denominationalism within Christianity is widely known and well documented. Even within orthodox Islam, it has been possible to develop a large number of 'sufi orders' to articulate the interests of various types of interest groups in Islamic countries. Within some of these sufi orders themselves, rival groupings can develop sometimes on the basis of the most trivial divergences in ritual details. (For detailed discussion of organisational articulation through religion, see the cases on pp. 102-6 below.)

Moral exclusiveness
In-group endogamy and the observance of exclusive group rituals can be of crucial importance in developing and maintaining the distinctiveness of the group in yet another respect. They both tend to generate the development of primary relationships among the members of the group and to inhibit the formation of such relationships with persons from outside the group. Marriage is nearly everywhere a means of establishing friendships and alliances between individuals and groups. When a group confines its marriages within itself then its members will become linked and cross-linked by primary relationships of patrilaterality, matrilaterality, affinity and of friendship. The Arab peasants say of such marriages that the children will have the same men as maternal and paternal uncles. Similarly, an exclusive cult will consolidate the distinctiveness of the group in the same way. Some cults employ

direct principles and techniques for encouraging primary interaction within the group and at the same time for inhibiting primary
interaction outside it. Essien-Udom (1966) shows how, in their
efforts to create 'the Nation of Islam', the Black Muslims in the
USA seek to insulate their members from social interaction with
outsiders and to intensify interaction among themselves, in order
to deepen the distinctiveness of the emerging nation. Again,
fraternising is an official principle of Freemasonic organisation and
a great deal of the time and resources of the lodges are devoted to
this end. Studies in contemporary societies have shown that
friendships, like marriages, tend to develop among the socially
equal. Interest groups enhance their distinctiveness by intensifying
friendly interaction within them and discouraging such interaction
with outsiders. In all these cases the primary relationships that
develop between members of a group are maintained and institutionalised by means of patterns of symbolic formations and activities, such as gifts exchange, gossip, play, ceremonials of all sorts,
and eating and drinking together. These patterns of symbolic
formations become an integral part of the culture of the group.

Style of life
Moral exclusiveness is often combined with the adoption of an
exclusive style of life whose symbolic formations distinguish the
group further from other groups and convince the members of the
group of their own special identity. The members of the group may
adopt some external distinguishing signs, like facial markings,
special hair styles, special clothes, uniforms, badges, ties and
regalia. They may live in an exclusive neighbourhood, distinct in
their housing style, furniture and decoration. They may also be
distinct from other groups in developing special manners, etiquette,
and speech accent. High status groups also enhance their distinctiveness through conspicuous consumption which, when carried to
extreme, becomes potlatching, leading to the destruction of wealth
to outprice and outpace other groups who cannot afford to do the
same. A club of wealthy men can exclude less fortunate men by
means of very high membership fees.

The symbolic strategies for solving the problem of distinctiveness
that have been briefly discussed here are isolated from one another
only analytically. In empirical reality they tend to be closely

SYMBOLIC STRATEGIES IN GROUP ORGANISATION

interconnected in different combinations. Under some circumstances one symbolic strategy like religion may be sufficient to achieve distinctiveness for a group, but often informal interest groups adopt a combination of strategies, to achieve the function of distinctiveness (see the cases in the next chapter). Also many predominantly formal groups adopt some of these informal mechanisms to supplement the formal arrangements in enhancing their distinctiveness.

2 COMMUNICATION

Distinctiveness alone will not convert a category of people into a functioning political group. A political group can develop and survive to the extent and within the limits of the development and maintenance of routine communication between its members. This is particularly important if the members of a group are scattered in different residential and employment places, as is often the case in large cities and in modern industrial society generally. Under these circumstances each member of the group may be involved in his struggle for power on his own and it is only when the members of the group exchange messages, pool their separate experiences, discuss their problems and identify the common denominators of these problems, that it is possible for them to develop a common policy and to coordinate their activities accordingly.

Some of the strategies of distinctiveness are often at the same time also strategies for communication. Ritual and ceremonial gatherings are everywhere occasions for communication and exchange of news and views between people. The chains of dyadic and of other forms of primary relationships that are brought about within the framework of kinship or by marriage or by friendship, i.e. all those mechanisms for the development of moral exclusiveness, form important pervasive channels for communication. Many of the traits making up the style of life of the group are another kind of 'language' for communication.

Communication need not be a face-to-face activity but can be mediated through key personalities such as religious functionaries, gossips, and special leaders.

3 DECISION-MAKING

Communication alone is not sufficient for a distinct group to act politically. The group must have some kind of procedure for the regular collection of political messages, for discussing them, and for deciding on appropriate action on them. Some political scientists differentiate three stages in the process of decision-making (see for example Macridis 1955). The first is the stage at which common problems are identified in the light of the information supplied through the channels of communication. This is followed by a stage of deliberation, when attempts are made to find solutions. In the final stage a decision is made on behalf of the whole group.

Thus, in the community of Hausa traders discussed below, laymen express their current anxieties in divination sessions with the *malams*. In their regular interaction among themselves the *malams* discuss the current problems that are afflicting the people. The senior *malams* discuss these problems with the leading traders and the chief in the course of consultation and divinatory sessions. In the course of these discussions the current problems confronting the community are formulated. This is followed by a stage of deliberation when in the course of theological discussions among the *malams* and in the course of divining sessions between the leading *malams* and the leading traders solutions are sought. Ultimately, the decisions are taken in that community by the '*hajjis*', i.e. the leading *malams* and traders whose leadership is validated in terms of pilgrimage to Mecca.

Similarly the practice and regulation of endogamy provide for many groups an important contribution to the process of decision-making. In the Arab lineage discussed below, one of the most significant roles played by the heads of the expanded families in their daily gatherings is related to the women of the group. The heads also deliberate on appropriate action by the lineage in cases relating to the honour of women. A woman always belongs to the lineage of her father. When she is married out, her father would tell those who marry her: 'For you the womb; for us the bone.' When she dies she ceases to be related to her husband and is claimed by her patrilineal kin. The husband will not be able to see her corpse and it will be her brother who will put her into the grave, not her husband. If she is harmed or if she commits adultery, it is her lineage who will take action. The lineage is very much 'the owner' of its women and issues affecting this ownership must be taken by responsible men within the group. An increase in the size of the group will not automatically weaken this concern of the men of the group for the movement of its women in marriage outside the group. In the south of the USA, in Rhodesia and in South Africa, the 'rape complex' has kept alive the jealousy of white men over 'the danger' to their women from the blacks and this has often been a contributory factor to the organisation of the group in throwing up 'leaders of opinion' who at the same time contribute to the taking of political decisions.

The process of decision-making may be conscious or unconscious. It may involve the participation of all members of the group or only part of the members. The decision may be by consensus or by majority, or it may be taken by a leader on behalf of the group.

4 AUTHORITY AND THE LEADERSHIP PROCESS

In dealing with the problem of decision-making we are dealing partly also with the problem of authority, though the two problems should be analytically separated. Decisions will be implemented if they are backed by authority and this involves the exercise of power. Authority therefore needs power: physical, or economic or normative.

Some informally organised groups may resort to physical violence to coerce members to comply with group decisions. But we are dealing here principally with groups operating within the framework of the modern state, where the state monopolises the regular use of physical coercion. Under these circumstances most informal interest groups have to mobilise mainly normative, symbolic power to support their authority structure.

The fact that the members of such a group share common interests does not mean that they will automatically act in conformity with the general interests of the group. This is because there is always opposition between the individual and the group to which he belongs in respect of rights and obligations. Men in general are always happy to claim their rights in the group but feel constrained when they are called upon to fulfil their obligations to the group. To use the terms of Fortes and Evans-Pritchard (1940), in its pragmatic and utilitarian aspects, the autonomy of the group is a source of immediate private interest and satisfaction to the individual. But as a common interest it is non-utilitarian and non-pragmatic, a matter of moral value and ideological significance. People are usually so preoccupied with their private interests that they do not always see the common interests on which they depend. Hence the necessity for exerting pressure on the individual to honour his obligations.

Authority can be collective as when a whole group will exercise pressure on the individual through gossip and scandal or through ostracism. But more often it is vested in one person or in a number of persons.

The organisation of authority is a difficult problem faced in all societies, simple and industrial, and by all groupings, formal and informal. As Duncan (1962) points out, all social order involves hierarchy and all hierarchy involves relations between superiors, inferiors and equals, and the mobility between these statuses. In both simple and industrial societies this is achieved by ceremonials. In most political groups, positions of authority are staffed by mortal people like you and me and it is a perpetual problem in society to elevate ordinary individuals to positions of 'semi-gods'. All the intellect, skill, and cunning of the ideologist, the politician, the theologian, and the artist and all the techniques of colour, music, poetry and drama are needed to create, accomplish and perpetuate the myth of authority in the face of continually subversive processes of different sorts.

This universality of the problem of authority and of the role of symbolic formations and symbolic action in meeting it comes out in a penetrating analysis by Fortes (1968) of the structural significance of the symbolic elements involved in the dramas of installation in roles, whether among the Ashanti of Ghana or among the English in Britain. The ceremonials employed in these dramas are necessary not only to impress the audiences of ordinary people with the transformed nature of the incumbents of the positions of authority, but also to prepare, groom, convince, and reassure the incumbents themselves of the reality of that transformation. Authority is an abstraction which can be seen only through its symbolism and ceremonials. This is to some extent true of even formally organised groups, where authority is backed mainly by contract. It is of course far more so in the case of informally organised groups.

The power behind authority is always composite, as it is derived from different kinds of social relations: political, economic, ritual and moral. Even in societies that are ruled by unpopular dictators, the rulers make use of power derived from networks of moral relationships or from beliefs in mystical forces.

Some groups articulate their authority in terms of a doctrine of intercession between mystical forces and ordinary people. In many sufi orders within Islam (including that of the Tijaniyya discussed on pp. 102-6 below) there is a chain of links between God, Muhammad, then down the list to the present ritual mediators, and masters. Sometimes the contemporary ritual intercessor is himself also the holder of authority in the group. More often, however, intercession may be vested in a ritual specialist who lends his support to the holder of authority.

Authority may also be associated with the possession of secret ritual formulae. Within Freemasonic organisations, initiation into the First Degree, then promotion to the Second, raising to the Third, and further promotion in the Royal Arch Degrees, are marked by the acquisition of more and more secret formulae. A Master is always addressed as 'Worshipful Master'. A Grand Master is addressed as the 'Most Worshipful Master'. In some ideologies of authority high office is associated with mystical powers that can cause harm through cursing or that can heal illness through blessing or through secret medicines.

Another source of power can be derived from a key position within a kinship or friendship network. In this case categorical imperatives that govern primary relationships between persons are mobilised to support persons in positions of authority.

Often different sources of power are mobilised together in different proportions to support authority. The fact that informal 'leadership' is not derived from the tangible forms of physical or economic power has led many scholars to explain it in terms of personality traits. The efforts of this school of thought, which has a very long ancestry, culminated in Weber's mystique of *charisma*, a quality of grace said to be given to some 'born leaders' and not to others.

In recent years, however, many scholars have found this view sociologically sterile and even misleading. A man may have all the traits of *charisma* without in fact becoming a leader. On the other hand, some men who are not particularly charismatic become or are even forced to become leaders. The same man may become a leader at one time but not at another.

Recent studies of leadership have tended to lay very little emphasis on the person, or persons who are dramatically singled out as leaders, and to concentrate instead on the leadership process – a process of mutual stimulation between the personalities of a collectivity.

This is because leadership is a group function and its analysis is possible only within the context of a group. The leadership process consists in the contribution by individuals towards the solution of the organisational problems of the group. This involves the mobilisation of old and new symbols, and their interpretation and reinterpretation. Some leaders distinguish themselves in one organisational field, acting for example as agents of communication, as decision-makers, as ideologists, as co-ordinators of group action, or as teachers-indoctrinators. Often, one individual may be capable of distinguishing himself in more than one of these organisational roles. As a group develops over time, different types of leaders may be needed at different stages of its development. Thus at an early stage 'founding leaders' may be particularly needed to bring about a consciousness of common interest in a collectivity, while at a later stage, when the distinctiveness of the group is already established, a leader-indoctrinator may be more acutely needed.

In all these cases the leaders fulfil their functions through the manipulation of symbols. At any one time, some symbolic forms can provide better solutions to the current problems of the group than others and those members who create, mobilise, or articulate them become potential leaders. It is the structural situation of the group that determines what type of symbols are more effective than others and hence what type of leader is needed. *Charisma* is largely a group function, not an individual trait. Underlying the symbolic process in the development of *charisma* is the creation of normative obligations which bind the members of the group together, both the leaders and the led. As a result, the leader is given by the group power which he exercises for the group. This power is normative in nature. It is essentially symbolic. The followers can with ease refuse to obey the leader without the fear of physical or economic sanctions.

5 IDEOLOGY

It is evident from the foregoing discussion that the articulation of the organisation of an informal group requires the mobilisation of different kinds of social relationships, the creation, strengthening and utilisation of different kinds of myths, beliefs, norms, values and motives. These different elements which are employed in the development of a political system become so interdependent that they tend to be seen in terms of an integrated ideological scheme which is related to the basic problems of man, his place in society and in the universe.

The compulsion for the development and maintenance of self-hood, and for finding solutions to the perennial problems of exist-ence, are expressed in terms of the symbolic forms that articulate the organisation of the interest group. Each of these elements lends support to the others and to the whole complex. Selfhood becomes identified in terms of membership of the group. The group and the self become parts in the scheme of the universe and are thereby validated.

Thus an ideology of this kind is not just a reflection of the various elements involved in the organisation of the group, but is itself a significant variable in its own right, contributing further to the development and functioning of the group. Once developed, it becomes an autonomous factor which can motivate people and impel them to action in its own right.

An important outcome of this integrative function of ideology is the economy it effects in our symbolic repertoire. Our life will be chaotic if we have to have separate symbolic patterns of behaviour for the development of our selfhood, for meeting the various peren-nial problems of our existence, for articulating each of the different organisational functions of each of our major groups. In such a situation we shall be completely lost in a jungle of symbols and our time and energy will be dissipated by endless performances. Further, the symbols will tend to become mere signs as they acquire a special meaning and their potency and effectiveness will thus be drastically reduced. What is more, the absence of the synchronising mechanisms of the ideology would have inevitably resulted in serious inconsistencies and incompatibilities between the various symbolic elements. In this way these elements would have weakened or even destroyed one another.

This integrative function of the ideology is the outcome of an ongoing process, involving the continual adjustment of numerous parts that are continually changing. New symbols may be created and old ones reinterpreted. The group may be changing in a variety of ways and the same may be the case with the other groups in the society or with the encapsulating system itself.

A great deal of unconscious modification of the ideology can take place through trial and error. But in the case of major political groupings there may emerge some ideological guardians and specialists. The charismatic leader, the philosopher, the theologian and the artist are continuously at work, seeking new symbolic formations, new 'theories', new interpretations, or new techniques of persuasion. These specialists will be in constant interaction with the members of the group and a great deal of mutual stimulation between them will occur.

An interest group may of course adopt a ready-made ideology instead of having to go through the costly and prolonged process of developing its own ideology. In the highly differentiated societies, ideologies tend to become specialisations and to be separated from the groups that initially created them. Newly developing groups can thus draw on these ideologies and it is not uncommon for the same ideology to be adopted by different groups for different purposes. But in all these cases the ready-made ideology is 'tailored' for the particular circumstances of the adopting group. This is made possible by the flexible nature of the symbols that are employed in the ideology.

6 BELIEF AND SYMBOLIC ACTION:
THE PROCESS OF SOCIALISATION

An ideology will function only if it is maintained and kept alive by continuous indoctrination, conditioning of moods and sentiments, and affirmation of belief. This is achieved mainly through ceremonials, in the course of which symbols are continuously charged with meanings that are relevant to the current problems of the group. Men are usually immersed in their day-to-day private problems and their immediate utilitarian interests, and they have therefore to be regularly shaken out of their egocentric concerns and made to reaffirm their belief in, and support of, the basic principles of their political organisation. The more elements of the political organisation that the ideology articulates the greater the need for frequent ceremonials. This is the case in all political organisations. But it is particularly so when a group is informally organised, when, because of the absence of the systematic use of organised physical coercion, increasing use is made of ritual and moral mechanisms.

Beliefs are rarely absolute in their hold on individuals or collectivities. There is always an element of doubt. This is partly because of the technical shortcomings of symbols and partly because of the essentially insoluble problems with which they grapple. Not all the members of the group will necessarily subscribe to the whole ideology of the group. Some will believe in some parts of the ideology and disbelieve in others. Other members may believe in the ideology, but would not like to say so in public. Yet others on the other hand do not ordinarily believe in it though they declare publicly that they do. What is certain, however, is what people actually do. It is related that the prophet Muhammad had said to his followers that what he was concerned with was that a good Muslim should pray five times a day. As to what went on in the mind of the worshipper, it was between him and Allah.

A senior Creole academician in Freetown told me that he did not subscribe to the beliefs contained in the traditional Creole cult of the dead. When his own father died he initially refused to go through the elaborate preparations and ceremonials that are prescribed by the cult. During the week between the occurrence of the death and the burial ceremony, I closely observed how step by step he was forced by pressures from various directions, from within his extended family and from within his status group, to go through all the obligatory ceremonials. I attended the funeral service at the cathedral in which well over a thousand men and women participated. Prayers were read, hymns were sung and a sermon given. I listened to one hymn in particular which said: 'There is a land that is fairer than light . . .'. It was sung by the whole congregation in a most skilful and moving way, accompanied by the organ which was played by a senior professional organist. The singing congregation were nearly all Christian, mainly Anglican, and they had been trained in choir singing since their childhood. They sang softly, beautifully, passionately and powerfully. The contrast between the grimness of death represented by the coffin in the middle of the cathedral, and the promised land which is 'fairer than light', to which the dead are supposed to go, was sharp. The genius of the poet, the skill of the organist, the art of the original composer of the music, the men and the women in their sober yet lavish clothes, the coffin and the trained voices of the congregation, combined to agitate the mind and to force one to think about the mysteries of life and death and about the destiny of man. I, who was neither Christian nor Creole, certainly experienced this and was certain that my friend, the academician, together with the rest of the congregation, experienced the same fit of agitation and contemplation. There was a feeling of some relief triggered by the promise of the bright land, which transformed the subjective experience from the dismal presence of death to a vista of hope.

This experience is vague and difficult to express. We must remember again that in dealing with a problem such as death we are dealing not with a purely empirical issue but with one of the perennial, irresolvable problems of human existence. The point that I am trying to emphasise is that if all the techniques of mystification were used to convince scientifically educated men that, for example, thunder is the angry voice of God, the men will never be convinced, because thunder can be explained empirically in a scientific way. But when these techniques are employed to persuade the same men to accept this or that explanation of a perennial problem like the meaning of death, that explanation or belief will be far more acceptable, since it will be expressing some deep inexpressible 'mystical' experience in vague and elusive terms.

Conviction may be only partial or even superficial, and it may be temporary. With most people, including saints and prophets, belief is seldom fixed and unshaken. The symbols that express and support belief always have technical shortcomings. There is thus a continuous interaction in the mind between individual experience, forms of belief and symbolic behaviour. One supports the other. Often it is the symbols and the ceremonials that conjure up belief, not the other way round. Symbols have no fixed meanings and can thus be differently interpreted at different times. This is why ritual and ceremonial are not once-and-for-all mechanisms, but have to be frequent and repetitive in order to do their job at all.

The problem of cultural heterogeneity

Each one of the organisational functions of the group is an aspect of the total relationships within the group. The different functions are highly interdependent and tend to support one another. A weakness in one function can be compensated for by the strengthening of another. For example, a group which has effective functions of communication can afford to have less effective functions of distinctiveness.

Similarly, the symbolic mechanisms that perform these functions are interdependent, supplementary, and to some extent substitutable. The same function can be achieved in terms of different symbolic forms and the same form can perform different functions. Often, different forms are combined in different ways to achieve different functions. But on the whole there is a tendency for different symbolic mechanisms to hang on together. As symbols tend to be used with great economy, a dominant symbolic form will tend to perform a good deal of the functions of the group. Thus, kinship relationships and their ceremonials can fulfil for a group the functions of distinctiveness, communication, authority, ideology and socialisation.

The symbolic mechanisms that are developed by a group to achieve its organisational functions comprise the culture of the group. The constraints that culture exerts on the individual come ultimately not from the culture itself, but from the collectivity of the group. It is the group that charges the symbols with their potency, often by exploiting the processes by which its members achieve selfhood and tackle the perennial problems of existence.

In a simple society with simple technology and little division of labour there can be said to be one homogeneous culture. But once a society develops beyond this elementary, rather hypothetical stage, different groups, each with its own culture or sub-culture, will emerge. Whether such a society will now be described as homogeneous or heterogeneous in its culture will depend on the social unit, the political grouping, that one takes as one's universe of reference. Even small primary groups develop their own peculiar norms and symbols which distinguish them from one another (see Argyle 1967). And when we take for our universe of research not a small group but, for example, an Indian village, then we are in fact considering a variety of groupings with markedly different patterns of symbolic forms. Thus, whether an Indian village is homogeneous or heterogeneous in its culture will depend on the unit of the study. If we study the different caste groups separately then each will have its own culture, articulating its own organisational functions. But if the unit of the study is the whole village, then the different cultures of the various groups will be seen as forming one culture

85

consisting of interrelated parts. In this way we can talk of the culture of a family, the culture of a class, a village, a province or the culture of a whole nation. A culture is thus a relative term, its identity being defined by a corporate interest group. In egalitarian societies with primitive technology there tend to be homologous groups with a homogeneous culture. But, once societies become differentiated as a result of the division of labour, a multiplicity of groups bearing different cultures will emerge.

In complex society different groups tend to have different cultural forms, including different styles of life and different ideologies. If we concentrate on the study of cultural forms on their own, then we shall have here a heterogeneity of culture. But if, as our studies develop, we progressively and accumulatively analyse cultural forms in terms of symbolic functions then the methodological problem of heterogeneity will be progressively overcome. This can be seen in a dramatic and clear way from a comparative survey of different ethnic groups in a modern society. As shown below (pp. 91-8), these are essentially interest groups that are informally organised. Some of them make extensive use of kinship symbols in articulating their organisational functions while others use religious symbols for the same purpose. All these groups, if they are of the same political level, seek to develop the same organisational functions, but do so in a variety of symbolic forms.

The analysis of symbolic forms in relation to symbolic functions which is the central problem of social anthropology can be greatly enhanced through comparing different cultural forms that are carried by different groups. Thus one aspect of our work is to reduce cultural heterogeneity to functional uniformities. This of course is an open problem for social anthropological research with which we progressively and systematically deal.

As increasingly more variables are isolated by analysis, as more effective techniques of field work and of processing field data have been evolved, and as a growing body of hypotheses about the nature of socio-cultural causation has been accumulated, these heuristic problems will be progressively overcome and need no longer restrict our field and our approach to it. This cumulative feature of our endeavour is indeed what we mean by describing social anthropology as a discipline.

Complex pluralism and the question of freedom

The picture given here of the informally organised group in modern society is unavoidably an oversimplification of what are highly complex, on-going politico-symbolic processes. The group has been considered on its own, in isolation from other groups. But modern society is pluralistic in its structure, consisting of a variety of groups that overlap, cut across, support, or oppose one another. Theoretically, each one of the major groups will attempt to impose its 'culture' and its own view of society and of the world on its members.

Two questions will immediately arise. First, how are the different groups related to one another so that society can function to some extent as an on-going system? Second, how does the individual person integrate within his psyche the different cultures and world views that are imposed on him by the different groups to which he belongs? These are interconnected questions and are in fact two aspects of the same problem.

The Evolutionists thought that this problem did not arise in 'primitive' society. In their polarised typology they presented 'primitive' society as a monolithically organised group within which, by implication, conflict did not occur. Man is dwarfed by the social structure and his personality and world-view are those of the group. In contrast, modern society is presented as being highly pluralistic and the same man is often affiliated to different groups. Because of this multiplicity of groupings, modern man is said to be more free than 'primitive' man because of the many options that are open to him in the conduct of his life.

But every student of social anthropology knows that nearly all simple societies are pluralistic too and social strife between groups within them as well as the conflict of loyalties within the individual self are endemic. He also knows that the principles of social organisation are often flexible and the individual can manoeuvre his course between different alternatives.

We also know that man in modern society is not as free in the choice of his groups of affiliation as the Evolutionists want us to believe. Consider the socio-cultural life of professionals and business men in a metropolis like London or New York. These are members of the middle classes who are said to be volatile, highly mobile, and hence very free. They are also highly educated and enlightened. And they live and work in what are probably some

87

of the most pluralistic and complex conurbation areas to be found anywhere in the world. Under such conditions these men must be the freest of men, in the sense that they have whole ranges of groups to choose from.

Yet, as we come down to empirical realities we realise that a good deal of this freedom of choice is illusory or exaggerated. A professional man has a specialised training which limits the range of his occupational mobility. He is obliged to belong to certain professional and occupational associations. His income is usually limited within a certain range and this often determines the type of house and the type of neighbourhood in which he lives. Like a vast number of other members of the middle classes, he most probably lives in suburbia and spends two or more hours a day commuting to and from work. Theoretically, the whole cultural world of London or New York is available for his enjoyment. But by the time he returns home from work, the baby-sitter arrives and he drives his wife to town to attend a performance it is often too late. Indeed I know many Londoners who hardly see the West End once in a year.

Similar circumstances circumscribe the world of the business executive or of the businessman. He is forced to belong to certain clubs, to associate with a narrow circle of friends, to marry a spouse from a narrow category of people. As I point out later, his style of life, patterns of behaviour and ideology are in fact an exclusive culture which envelops him and constrain his action. And the higher the social status of the man, the heavier the burden of the ceremonials, conventions, etiquette and other types of symbolic behaviour that are necessary to develop and uphold that status.

The overwhelming majority of men in the modern pluralistic society live within small areas of social life and are forced to stick to their jobs. Their economic interests and the groupings formed on the basis of these interests condition their lives to a very large extent. Indeed this is so much so that scholars like Riesman *et al.* (1950) and Marcuse (1964) argue that, as modern society develops, fewer and fewer, but larger and stronger, corporations come to dominate our social and cultural life and put an end to our freedom.

The Hausa man of Northern Nigeria enjoyed, even in pre-colonial days, a degree of freedom of choice which is in no way inferior to that of contemporary industrial man. He was geographically mobile, particularly during the dry season, and could move from village to village and from country to country. He was also occupationally mobile, engaging part of the time in trade and the other part in agriculture. When his business fortunes were at an ebb, he posed as an Islamic teacher, diviner, barber, butcher, commission agent, porter or beggar. He could even in a sense change parents and relatives through the extensive institutionalised practice of fostering. And, while our academician or businessman in industrial society can marry only one wife at a time, our traditional Hausa man could marry up to four wives and could also enjoy, without much shame or embarrassment, sexual and social intimacies with many concubines.

Thus man in simple societies is not as monolithic, and modern man not as pluralistic, as the Evolutionists argue. But while stating this I do not want to go to the other extreme by dismissing the differences between the small-scale, subsistence level society and the large-scale, technologically advanced society. It is however evident that both kinds of society are pluralistic and in both there are quarrels as well as co-operation between groups. In both, men are frequently torn by conflicting loyalties derived from memberships in disparate groupings.

Anthropologists have analysed many mechanisms for the regulation of inter-group relations in simple societies. Even the feud – a state of permanent enmity between groups and individuals – has its rules and regulations. Marriage regulations, friendships, ritual, institutionalised exchange of insults (known as joking relationships), these and many other cultural mechanisms develop between potentially conflicting groups and link them to one another.

As Smith (1956) points out, all societies are segmentary in their structure and people who are enemies on one level are allies on a different level. The very mechanisms that are employed in the organisation of a group are at the same time mechanisms for bringing into a unity smaller groups. In all groups, whether formal or informal, whether in simple or in modern society, there are mechanisms for tension-reduction that aim at uniting disparate individuals and groupings for co-ordinated action. Within the individual psyche, there are corresponding psycho-cultural mechanisms that work to integrate the ideologies of the different groups in which the individual is a member, to relate the variety of roles that he plays to one another within the framework of the same psyche or self.

'Invisible' organisations: 6
some case studies

Ethnic groups
Élite groups
Religious groups
Secret ritual groups
Cousinhoods

A good deal of sociological literature on the significance of informal interaction and informal groupings in western societies is available. Ever since the 'rediscovery of the primary group' there have been extensive studies of the development and functioning of informal relationships within on-going, rationally organised bureaucratic structures. Within political science there have been a number of studies of community power structures, particularly those of business. Still more extensive studies have been made by a large number of sociologists of the relation between religion and politics. There are certainly many useful insights, observations and hypotheses that can be found in this literature.

On the whole, however, the systematic study of informally

organised interest groups in modern society is still in its infancy. Many such groups remain unidentified and in many cases their members are not aware of their membership or of the very existence of the groups to which they belong. In many cases a correlation is established between certain symbolic patterns of behaviour and certain political groupings but without any analysis of *how* the two spheres are related and *how* they affect one another. As Geertz (1966) points out this last weakness is also evident in social anthropology.

In what follows, I give a brief account of some case studies, including three from my own works, of a variety of informally organised interest groups operating within modern political contexts in both developing and developed societies: ethnic groups, élite groups, ritual groups, groups with secret patterns of symbolic action, and groups organised as cousinhoods. In each case, there are structural circumstances that prevent the group from organising itself as a formal association. In each case one or another of the patterns of symbolic formations discussed in the previous chapter is exploited to solve organisational problems for the group. All the groups discussed can be described as 'culture groups' in the sense of each having a special style of life or a special combination of a variety of symbolic formations, that distinguish it from the rest of the society. Most of the groups discussed make use of nearly all the different symbolic strategies discussed earlier, though sometimes using one symbolic strategy as an articulating mechanism. In some of the cases I show how a group shifts in articulating its organisational mechanisms from one major symbolic form to another. Though they differ in their cultural forms they are structurally the same, being interest groups co-ordinating their corporate action in terms of an informal organisation.

Ethnic groups

There is now a rapidly accumulating literature demonstrating how under certain circumstances some interest groups exploit parts of their traditional culture in order to articulate informal organisational functions that are used in the struggle of these groups for power within the framework of formal organisations (see, for example, Caplan 1970 and Parkin 1974). In African studies this phenomenon has been labelled as 'tribalism' while in general sociological studies it has been labelled as 'ethnicity'.

An ethnic group is a collectivity of people who share some patterns of normative behaviour, or culture, and who form a part of a larger population, interacting within the framework of a common social system like the state. The term ethnicity refers to the degree of conformity to these collective norms in the course of social interaction.

It is obvious that this definition is so wide that it covers collectivities that are not usually described as 'ethnic'. This is a crucially important sociological issue which will be clarified later on in the course of the analysis.

Some dramatic cases of ethnic politics have been reported recently from modern African societies. In the early 1920s two distinct tribal groups of migrant 'strangers' developed in the city of Ibadan, capital of Yorubaland in Nigeria: those of the Hausa and of the Western Ibo. In conformity with the principles and practices of the so-called 'indirect rule' system of government, the British colonial administration recognised the distinctiveness of these tribal groups, protected them, and encouraged them to develop their own systems of administration, their own social and cultural autonomy. Each group was allotted a separate territorial settlement, a 'village', which later, as the city grew in size, became a special quarter in it. The Hausa quarter came to be known as 'Sabo' and that of the Western Ibo came to be known as 'Ekotedo'. In both communities a tribal chief was appointed and tribal customs in such matters as marriage, inheritance and religion were maintained. Both had a similar start and equal opportunity to develop their own separate distinctiveness, institutions and style of life.

When I carried out field study in Ibadan in 1963, nearly forty years later, the two ethnic groups presented a picture of sharp contrast. The Hausa had not only preserved their distinctiveness but also deepened their cultural identity and exclusiveness. They spoke only Hausa and interacted socially, as friends and relatives, only among themselves. A tense cleavage existed between them and some sections of the host population, brought about by continuous quarrels and hostility. The Western Ibo, on the other hand, had lost their socio-cultural autonomy. As Okonjo (1967) shows, their residential segregation had completely broken down and their compounds were occupied by people from different ethnic groups. They did have a tribal association, 'The Western Ibo Union of Ibadan', but it was a weak association, met only once a month, and had often suffered from the embezzlement of its funds and from the frequent quarrels among its members. Like many other tribal associations in Africa, the Western Ibo Union aimed, not at the development of an exclusive ethnic polity but, on the contrary, at promoting the successful adaptation of its members to modern urban conditions. As is well known, affiliation to such formal tribal association is often only a temporary measure taken by new migrants to the city to get help to adjust to the new social milieu. Second generation Western Ibos spoke Yoruba without accent and had Yoruba as their playmates.

These two ethnic groups in Ibadan represent the two extreme ends of a continuum found throughout Africa today. The one end of ethnic groups rapidly losing their cultural distinctiveness and the other of ethnic groups not only retaining but also emphasising and exaggerating their socio-cultural autonomy. In the one case an ethnic group adjusts to the new social realities by adopting customs from other groups or by developing new customs which are shared with other groups. In the second case an ethnic group adjusts to the new realities by reorganising its own traditional customs, or by developing new customs under traditional symbols, often using traditional norms and ideologies to enhance its distinctiveness within the dynamic contemporary situation.

This difference in the reaction of ethnic groups to modern conditions has been explained by some writers, both western and African, in terms of 'modernist-conservative' tendencies. Ethnicity is thus regarded as a symptom of reaction, ignorance and primitivity. Migrants from allegedly conservative societies, like that of the Hausa, are thought to tend to develop exclusive groupings while migrants from 'dynamic cultures', like that of the Western Ibo, are said to tend towards the rapid integration of their members within the modern socio-cultural context.

But even the most backward of men do not fight or kill one another simply because they are culturally different. On the other hand, even in some of the most advanced industrial western societies men sometimes divide on ethnic lines, such as the cleavage between Protestant and Catholic in Northern Ireland, or that between the Welsh and the English in southern Britain, and engage in bitter disputes which occasionally lead to violence and bloodshed. Indeed the sociological evidence from the USA indicates that some highly educated and economically differentiated ethnic groups have not only preserved but even in some cases revived and consolidated their ethnic distinctiveness. The Creoles of Sierra Leone, among whom I carried out field study, are one of the most highly educated and culturally westernised élite groups to be found anywhere. Yet, they constitute an ethnic group which for long has been in continuous competition and struggle for power with other ethnic groups in the country.

Other scholars have interpreted the difference in terms of variations in the type of cultural tradition. Thus some anthropologists have argued that migrant ethnic groups who come from segmentary societies, i.e. uncentralised polities, are particularly predisposed to the formation of formal tribal associations while those who come from centralised societies are not.

There is no doubt that traditional customs contribute significantly to the type of grouping that migrants develop. The Hausa of Sabo themselves explain their ethnic exclusiveness by repeatedly pointing out that their customs are different. But the culture and system of social relationships among these Hausa are far from being reproductions of the culture and social system in Hausaland in northern Nigeria. Indeed, not all Hausa migrants into Yorubaland have found it necessary to live within autonomous Hausa communities. Tens of thousands of Hausa who migrate annually to southern Nigeria to seek seasonal employment live in small, scattered, loosely knit gangs of workers without forming or joining organised communities. Hausa cultural tradition, therefore, is not the crucial factor in the formation of exclusive Hausa groupings in Yoruba towns.

Men may and do certainly joke about or ridicule the strange and bizarre customs of men from other ethnic groups, because those customs are different from their own. But they do not fight over such differences alone. When men *do*, on the other hand, fight across ethnic lines it is nearly always the case that they fight over some fundamental issues concerning the distribution and exercise of power, whether economic, political, or both, within the social system in which they take part.

The Western Ibos in Ibadan, as Okonjo points out, can be found scattered in places of employment all over the town. They are occupationally differentiated, ranging from university lecturers, through mechanics, clerks and printers, to workers of all sorts. Their distinctiveness is thus sharply weakened or made unnecessary by the new occupational and class cleavages that cut across their ethnic boundaries.

A study of the Sabo community and of other Hausa communities in Yoruba towns, on the other hand, shows that their development and their structure are closely interconnected with the development and organisational requirements of long-distance trade between the savannah and the forest belt, in which most of their members are directly or indirectly engaged. Under the pre-industrial conditions prevailing in Nigeria, long-distance trade is attended by a number of technical problems which can be effectively overcome when men from one ethnic group, speaking the same language and observing the same code of conduct, control all or most of the stages of the trade in specific commodities. Such an ethnic control, or monopoly, can usually be achieved only in the course of continual and bitter rivalry with competitors from other tribes. In the process, the monopolising ethnic community is forced to organise for political action in order to deal effectively with increasing external pressure, to co-ordinate the co-operation of its members in the common cause, and to mobilise the support of communities from the same ethnic stock in neighbouring towns.

When, in a hypothetical case, two ethnic groups join together and interact politically and economically and establish a new political system, they will soon become involved in cleavages on economic and political lines running throughout the extent of the new society. If a new line of cleavage, such as that of social class, will cut across ethnic lines, then ethnic identity and exclusiveness will tend to be inhibited by the emerging countervailing alignments. The poor from the one ethnic group will co-operate with the poor from the other ethnic group against the wealthy from both ethnic groups, who will, on their part, also co-operate in the course of the struggle to maintain their privileges. If the situation develops in this way, tribal differences will weaken and eventually disappear. The people will become detribalised. In time the class division will be so deep that two sub-cultures, with different styles of life, will develop and we may have a situation similar to that of Victorian Britain, to which Disraeli referred as 'the two nations', meaning the privileged and the underprivileged.

But the situation will be entirely different if the new class cleavage in our hypothetical example will coincide with tribal affiliations, so that within the new system the privileged will tend

95

to be identified with one tribal group and the underprivileged with the other tribal group. In this situation cultural differences between the two groups will become entrenched, consolidated and strengthened in order to articulate the struggle between the two social groups across the new class lines. Old customs will tend to persist. But within the newly emerging social system they will assume new values and new social significance. A great deal of social change will take place, but will tend to be effected through the rearrangement of traditional cultural items, rather than through the development of new cultural items, or, more significantly, rather than the borrowing of such items from the other tribal groups. Thus to the casual observer it will look as if there is here stagnation, conservatism, or a return to the past, when in fact we are confronted by an essentially new social system in which men articulate their new roles under traditional tribal symbols. This is why a concentration on the study of culture as such will shed little light on the nature of this kind of situation. For culture is not an independent system, but is a collection of diverse types of norms, values, beliefs, practices and symbols which, though affecting one another, are largely systematised, or structured, in social situations. Ethnicity therefore can be understood only when it is analysed within the contexts of new social situations. On the whole, a tribal group, or indeed any group, in the town should be seen in two distinct but highly interrelated dimensions: the political and the cultural.

On the basis of the foregoing discussion, some major points can be made about the nature of ethnicity.

Ethnicity in modern society is the outcome of intensive *interaction* between different culture groups, and not the result of a tendency to separatism. It is the result of intensive struggle between groups over new strategic positions of power within the structure of the new state: places of employment, taxation, funds for development, education, political positions and so on. In many places the possibilities of capturing these new sources of power have been different for different ethnic groups, so that very often the emerging cleavages have been on ethnic lines. As a result of this intensified struggle, many ethnic groups mobilise their forces and search for ways in which they can organise themselves politically so as to conduct their struggle more effectively. In the processes of this mobilisation a new emphasis is placed on parts of their traditional culture and this gives the impression that there is here a return to tribal tradition and to tribal separatism when in fact 'tribalism', or ethnicity, in the contemporary situation is one type of political grouping within the framework of the new state.

Ethnicity involves a dynamic rearrangement of relations and of customs and is not the result of cultural conservatism or continuity. The continuities of customs and of some social formations are certainly there, but their symbolic functions have changed. As Gluckman points out (1942:65) 'where in a changing system the dominant cleavage is into two culture groups, each of these groups will tend to set increasingly greater value on its own endo-culture, since this expresses the dominant cleavage'.

Ethnicity is fundamentally a political phenomenon, as the symbols of the traditional culture are used as mechanisms for the articulation of political alignments. It is a type of informal interest grouping. It does not form part of the formal structure of the state. If an ethnic group is formally recognised by a state, for example within a federation, then it is no longer an ethnic group, but a province or a region. Ethnicity differs, on the other hand, from formal associations in that an ethnic group has no explicitly stated aims and is not rationally and bureaucratically organised. An ethnic group is thus sociologically different from an ethnic association, just as caste is different from caste association.

Ethnicity can be found in all countries today, both the developed and the underdeveloped, and there is extensive sociological literature on it, including a large number of case studies, particularly in the USA. For example, in their now classic study, *Beyond the Melting Pot*, Glazer and Moynihan (1965) describe how in New York City, while the Scandinavians and the Germans have been assimilated into the main body of white Anglo-Saxon Protestants, the Negroes, Puerto Ricans, Jews, Italians and Irish have remained distinct because these latter groups are associated with distinct occupational and status interests. In a recent survey, Hannerz (1974) describes how ethnicity helped in the development and maintenance of large-scale criminal organisations in the USA. In the same way, ethnicity enabled Hausa thieves to organise and operate in Ibadan and also made it possible for thousands of Hausa men to dominate the highly organised and lucrative begging industry in West Africa (Cohen 1969b).

Ethnicity provides an array of symbolic strategies for solving most or all of the basic problems of organisational articulation. The

97

cultural identity of the group provides the major mechanism for distinctiveness. The tendency for the ethnic group to be highly endogamous distinguishes the group further in creating an exclusive network of patrilateral, matrilateral and affinal relationships and thereby enclosing a great deal of primary relationships within the group and inhibiting the formation of such relationships with people from outside the group. Even when the group goes through a process of change, it will adjust to the new situation in terms of its own traditional customs without adopting customs shared with members of other groups. The dense network of kinship and affinity created by endogamous marriages within the group will enhance the distinctiveness of the group further by transforming it into a 'bilateral descent group', whose members can claim sharing a common 'origin' or being from 'the same stock'.

These symbols of distinctiveness will serve at the same time as channels for communication. They will also help in articulating an authority structure by mobilising kinship, friendship and religious obligations in support of an informal authority agency. Similarly, the hierarchies within religious congregations and organs for welfare and mutual help can become vehicles for the routinisation of decision-making procedures. The symbols providing these organisational mechanisms are ideologically integrated within such mottoes as 'our customs are different', 'the sacredness of our traditions', and so on. The ideology is further elaborated to cover a narrative 'historical' account of the origin, the goings and comings, of the group. Finally, through the continual observance of the customs and ceremonies peculiar to the group, the members are continually socialised in the culture of the group.

Élite groups

To highlight some of the sociological issues raised by the analysis of organisational articulation through ethnicity, I discuss now a different kind of informal grouping, considered this time within the context of such a complex and highly industrialised society as Britain. I shall not choose an apt illustration, such as Protestant and Catholic groupings in Northern Ireland or the formation of ethnic immigrant communities in many parts of the country, but a highly formalised and bureaucratised structure which is officially governed by purely contractual mechanisms. I am referring here to the now widely known case of the economic élite, or élites, who dominate the City of London, the nerve centre of the financial system of Britain. No field work by professional anthropologists or sociologists has been carried out in the City, but in recent years, and particularly since the publication of the *Report of the Bank Rate Tribunal* in 1958, some accounts of various features of the organisation of business in it have emerged from a number of publications (see Lupton and Wilson 1959; Ferris 1960; Sampson 1962; Chapman 1968; Parry 1969).

From these accounts it is evident that millions of pounds worth of business is conducted daily in the City without the use of written documents, mainly verbally in face-to-face conversations or through the telephone. This is said to be technically necessary if business is to flow. But as the risks involved are formidable, the business is confined within a limited number of people who trust one another. Such a high degree of trust can arise only among men who know one another, whose values are similar, who speak the same language in the same accent, respect the same norms and are involved in a network of primary relationships that are governed by the same values and the same patterns of symbolic behaviour.

For these reasons, City men are recruited from some exclusive status groups. They are mostly products of the English public-school system. The schools in this system achieve two major tasks: first, they socialise, or rather train, their pupils in specific patterns of symbolic behaviour, including accent, manner of speech, etiquette, style of joking, play. Second, they create a web of enduring friendship and comradeship among the pupils and these relationships are often continued after graduation through periodic old-boy unions, affiliation within the same clubs, and further interaction in other social situations.

The City is said to be a village – barely one square mile in territory – in which everyone of importance knows everyone of importance. Who you know is more important than what you know. Often, the élite of the City are related to one another not only by a common style of life and by friendship, but also by kinship and affinal relationships. Lupton and Wilson (1959) present a construction of the genealogies of over twenty élite family groupings that are interrelated through marriage and show the connections between top administrative, financial and industrial 'decision-makers'.

The available reports indicate strongly that the speed and efficiency with which the City conducts its business are made possible mainly by this network of primary, informal, relationships connecting the business élite. This network is governed by archaic norms, values and codes that are derived from the City's 'tribal past' – as Sampson puts it. It is held together by a complex body of customs that are to an outsider as esoteric and bizarre as those in any foreign culture. Ferris (1960:58–74) gives a dramatic description of the odd and highly stylised manner in which the stockbrokers – known in the City as the Top-Hatters (because they still wear top hats) make their daily rounds in the City. They queue at a bank on a hard bench, their striped trousers tugged up, exchanging a copy of *The Times* for one of the *Daily Telegraph*. When they see the bank official, they pull up a chair and talk about cricket, television and politics before any mention of the word money. This business of How-do-you-do, Ferris was told, is to say in effect: 'We accept the normal rules of society, and we can now start exchanging ideas.' 'If you go to a bank with a top hat they say: "Oh, it's one of the brokers", and you walk right in. If you went in in a homburg there'd be an awful business of "Good gracious me, Mr. –, where's your hat this morning?" There'd be a *thing*, which of course you want to avoid at all costs.' For if you behave in an 'abnormal' manner, your bank official will think that there is something 'fishy' about your behaviour and unless there is an obvious explanation, your creditworthiness may suffer. Without unblemished trustworthiness a broker cannot operate.

The Hausa traders in Yoruba towns, discussed in the last section, conduct their business in much the same way as the City men, though they operate under different structural circumstances and using different symbolic patterns. A Hausa dealer from northern Nigeria will entrust his goods and money in the south only to a Hausa broker. No matter how long the Hausa broker has been living in a Yoruba town in the south he will always be anxious to preserve the symbols of his Hausaism, dressing like a Hausa, speaking and behaving like a Hausa. Hausaism is essential for his livelihood. Just as City men in London make use of a series of customs to overcome technical problems of business, so do the Hausa use different Hausa customs to create relationships of trust in the trading network. The customs that are implicit in the life style of the City men, are as sovereign in their constraining power as are the customs implicit in Hausa culture

City men constitute an interest group which is part of the system of the division of labour in British society. They use their connections and the symbolism of their life style to articulate a corporate organisation which is partly formal and partly informal, in order to compete within the wider social system for a greater share of the national income. So do the Hausa use their culture to organise and co-ordinate their effort in order to maintain their share of the profits. In short, City men are socio-culturally as distinct within British society as are the Hausa within Yoruba society. They are indeed as 'ethnic' as any ethnic group can be. But they are not usually described as an ethnic group because the term 'ethnic' connotes to many people lower status, minority status, or migrancy. Numerically, City men are literally a minority. But largely because of their high and privileged status they are referred to as 'élite', not a 'minority'.

Here lies the sociological significance of the study of the politics of ethnicity. Ethnicity throws into relief, or rather dramatises the processes by which the symbolic patterns of behaviour implicit in the style of life, or in the 'sub-culture' of a group – even of highly individualistic men like an élite – develop in order to articulate organisational functions that cannot be formally institutionalised. It is easy to identify an élite when its men are from an ethnically distinct group like the Creoles in Sierra Leone, the Americo Liberians in Liberia, or the Tutsi in Ruanda. But it is difficult to do so with an élite whose cultural distinctiveness within the society is not so visible, and whose members appear to the casual observer to be highly independent individualists.

To conclude, although an élite may share the same basic culture of the society in which they live, they achieve distinctiveness in terms of their special style of life (accent, dress, manners, patterns of friendship, exclusive gatherings, élite endogamy and ideology). They communicate informally through exclusive gatherings within different types of frameworks such as old-school meetings and private clubs. Through these channels of communication they identify their corporate problems, deliberate over them, and take decisions. Compliance with these decisions is ensured by the various types of constraints that are built into the symbolic complexes of their social networks and their style of life generally.

They validate their élite position in terms of an ideology, or a 'theory', which is designed to convince the ordinary members of the society, as well as themselves, of the legitimacy of their status. The ceremonials that pervade their lives in all sorts of situations keep alive this ideology and repetitively augment its symbols with meanings. Some members of the élite will usually specialise in the elaboration of their ideology, while other members will specialise in the art of staging ceremonials to keep their symbols alive. Thus, although they ostensibly appear as separate and distinct individuals in different fields of life without obvious corporate organisation, the élite achieve organisational co-ordination informally through the symbolic blue-print of the style of life which they share with one another.

Religious groups

An interest group will usually exploit many symbolic forms in the construction of its organisation: kinship and marriage, language, style of life. In the process of the mobilisation and integration of these forms within a unified ideology, one of them may become dominant as an 'articulating principle'. Which form will predominate in this way in the organisation of the group will depend on a variety of circumstances, both within the group and outside it within the encapsulating political system. It will also depend on the flexibility and potency of its major symbols. Some symbolic forms have greater potentialities for becoming articulating principles than others. One of these is religion. I shall discuss the processes of its development as an articulating institution by examining some particular cases from Africa and the USA.

Under the protective umbrella of indirect rule in the former colonial territories of Africa, many ethnic groups developed corporate economic and political interests of their own and their distinctiveness became a vital vested interest shared by most of their members. But with the rise and development of nationalist movements after the Second World War in these territories and, finally with independence, indirect rule came to an end. A direct threat to the corporateness, and hence to the common interests, of these groups developed. Their distinctiveness was no longer officially recognised. Indeed in many cases this basis was declared to be incompatible with national unity, independence and equality of citizenship. Furthermore, with the withdrawal of official recognition and support by the colonial administration, the structure and legitimacy of traditional authority within them were undermined.

Most of these groups struggled hard to adjust to the new conditions. Some of them succeeded in reorganising their corporateness on new political lines that were in conformity with the new political realities. But others, who could not do so effectively, began to articulate their organisation informally, in many cases in terms of religious symbols. This can be seen in a dramatic form in the recent history of the Hausa community in Ibadan which I discussed earlier in this chapter. With the coming of party politics in Nigeria in the early 1950s, along with the rise of Nigerian nationalist movement and subsequently of independence, the whole basis of Hausa distinctiveness was undermined. Their community was no longer officially recognised as an exclusive 'tribal' group and the support which had been given by the colonial government to the authority of the Hausa chief was withdrawn. The weakening position of the chief affected not only the organisation of the functions of communication, decision-making, and co-ordination of policy within the quarter, but also the very distinctiveness of the community because it was no longer possible for the chief to coerce individuals to act in conformity with the corporate interests of the group.

In the meantime, the ethnic exclusiveness of the community was being threatened by increasing social interaction between Hausa and Yoruba in two major social fields: party politics and joint Islamic rituals and ceremonials. Interaction of this kind was creating primary moral relationships between Hausa and Yoruba, under new values, norms and symbols.

It was at this juncture that a major revolution in the quarter's religion took place when the overwhelming majority of its men were initiated into a mystical Islamic sufi brotherhood called the Tijaniyya. The Tijaniyya brought about fundamental changes in the organisation of the quarter's religion. First it localised the daily ritual through the obligatory principle that an initiate should perform at least the evening major rituals under his own master who initiated him into the order. This meant that the Hausa no longer went to pray together with Yoruba in Yoruba mosques in the town. In addition, the community seceded from the Yoruba

Central Mosque by deciding to hold the Friday mid-day prayer in the central mosque in the quarter, under the leadership of the quarter's chief and chief Imam, against the bitter opposition of the Yoruba Imamate (see below pp. 133-4).

Second, the Tijaniyya greatly intensified ritual by the addition of special ritual duties to the ordinary five daily prayers of Islam. An average Tijani would thus spend on ritual duties about an hour and twenty minutes on a weekday and three-and-a-half hours on Friday.

Third, the Tijaniyya collectivised ritual in the quarter and thus created new ritual groupings.

The adoption of the Tijaniyya by the quarter brought about processes which halted the disintegration of the bases of the exclusiveness and identity of the quarter. The reorganisation of the quarter's religion was at the same time a reorganisation of the quarter's political organisation. A new myth of distinctiveness for the quarter was founded. The community was now a superior, puritanical, ritual community, a religious brotherhood distinct from the masses of Yoruba Muslims in the city, complete with their separate Friday mosque, Friday congregation and a separate cemetery.

The localisation of ritual in the quarter inhibited the development of much social interaction with the Yoruba. On the other hand the intensification and collectivisation of ritual increased the informal social interaction within the quarter, under Hausa traditional values, norms, and customs.

The Tijaniyya also introduced the principle of intercession according to which the sacred emanation of Allah, the *baraka*, is mediated to members of the order through a chain of ritual masters and saints. A Tijani is therefore dependent on his master who initiated him into the order, gave him his ritual instructions and thus became the direct link between the initiate and the higher ritual mediators, through to the founder of the order, to the Prophet, and ultimately to Allah. The *malams* thus became the sole mediators between laymen and Allah, in whom all the mystical forces of the universe are concentrated. Through their services as teachers, interpreters of the dogma, ritual masters, diviners, magicians, spiritual healers, and officiants in rites of passage, the *malams* developed multiple relationships of power over laymen and, through the hierarchy of ritual authority instituted by the order, this power is finally concentrated in the hands of the big *malams*.

Through their manifold relationships with the business land-lords and the chief, the big *malams* have become part of the estab-lishment. They act as advisers to the landlords and the chief and they formally participate in the formulation of problems, in deliberation, and decision-making, and in the co-ordination of action in matters of general policy. They also play significant roles in the processes of communication and co-ordination in the course of the routine administration of the quarter.

Many ethnic groups in African towns organise themselves in terms of a religious ideology, in the form of a separatist church, an exclusive mystical order, or of some other type of cult. Similar phenomena can be found in other parts of the world. In the USA, many interest groups that in the past articulated their organisation in terms of ethnicity have now shifted to religion as an organising principle. Glazer and Moynihan (1965) state that in New York 'religious institutions are generally closely linked to distinct ethnic groups' and that most ethnic groups have religious names. This may explain the nature of the so-called religious paradox in the USA today when increasing secularisation goes together with increasing affiliation within religious organisations. Herberg (1960:3) states: 'Americans think, feel, and act in terms quite obviously secularist at the very time that they exhibit every sign of a widespread religious revival.' Lenski (1963:319–66), on the basis of intensive studies of religion in Detroit, detects 'a trend toward increased religious group communalism' and states that 'the successor to the ethnic sub-community is the socio-religious sub-community, a group united by ties of race and religion'. Large sections of lower-class blacks have in recent years organised themselves in terms of a religious ideology and organisation and are known as the Black Muslims. Essien-Udom (1966) shows how in their efforts to create the 'Nation of Islam', the Black Muslims insulate their members from much interaction with whites and with non-Muslim blacks, while at the same time put pressure on members to intensify interaction among themselves in order to deepen the distinctiveness of the emerging 'nation'. Communication is effected through the theocratic politico-ritual hierarchy running from the head of the movement, the Messenger, down to his ministers, who are in charge of the local temples, then down the hierarchy to the captains, secretary, treasurers and investigators.

Religion provides an ideal 'blue-print' for the articulation of informal organisation for interest groups. It mobilises powerful emotions and sentiments that are associated with the basic problems of human existence and gives legitimacy and stability to political arrangements by representing these as a natural part of the system of the universe. It makes it possible to use the arrangements for financing and administering places of worship and associated places for welfare, education, and social activities of various sorts, to use these in developing the organisation of political functions. It also provides frequent and regular meetings in congregations, where in the course of ritual activities, a great deal of informal interaction takes place, information is communicated and general problems are formulated and discussed and decisions taken. The system of myths and symbols which religion provides is given to interpretation and reinterpretation and can thus be accommodated to changing economic, political, and other social circumstances, serving as a flexible ideology for the group.

Secret ritual groups

Another institution which has been manipulated for the articulation of the informal organisation of interest groups is the secret ritual society. There are various types of secret societies all over the world in both the developed and the developing countries. They differ in their methods of recruitment, some being voluntary while others are compulsory. They also differ in what is kept secret and what is made public. In some, membership is secret, but the rituals are not. In others, membership is public knowledge but the rituals are secret. Most varieties are unisexual in membership, with male secret societies being more widespread than those of females.

One of these secret societies is Freemasonry, which has been described as the largest secret society in the world, having a membership of about six million men, mostly from the wealthy and professional classes in the advanced industrial societies of the West. There are four million in the USA and three-quarters of a million in Britain. Formally, membership in the movement is not secret, but the rituals are secret. In reality, hardly anything is known about membership, but everything is now known about the rituals.

While the doctrine, rituals and organisation of this fraternity are nearly the same everywhere, their social functions and involvement in the distribution and maintenance of power are different under different circumstances. In some cases the movement seems to integrate occupational groups, in others classes, élites, opposition movements, right-wing movements – i.e. principally groupings that cannot be fully organised in formal associations.

This does not mean that men join the fraternity because of its function in organising interest groups. Most of them join for purely individual considerations. The political functions of the fraternity are often unintended and even unconscious.

One way in which we can learn about the manner in which this movement articulates the informal organisation of an interest group is to study its structure and activities within a small-scale developing society. There is hardly a country in the Third World where no Freemasonic lodges exist. Sierra Leone is a case in point. Here, the fraternity is concentrated in the capital, Freetown, where about two thousand members are affiliated within seventeen lodges. Apart from a few non-Sierra Leoneans, all the members are Africans, mainly from a group known as the Creoles.

The Creoles are the descendants of African slaves who were emancipated by the British early in the nineteenth century and were duly settled in the Freetown peninsula. From the very beginning of their settlement in their new home, the Creoles made a bid to start a new cultural life. Within a few decades they became very highly anglicised in their names, religion, style of dress, food, housing, education, and for a while they became known as 'Black Englishmen'. They are predominantly literate, highly educated and occupationally differentiated.

Although they are only 1.9 per cent of the population of Sierra Leone, they dominate the civil service, the judiciary and the professions of medicine, law, engineering, teaching and others. They also own the bulk of the freehold land in the Freetown peninsula. From these two sources of income and wealth they have developed into an élite, highly privileged, group within the country.

But with the rise of the Sierra Leone nationalist movement and later of independence, these two strongholds of Creole power have been challenged by the tribesmen of the provinces, particularly by the two powerful groups, the Mende and the Temne, each comprising about 30 per cent of the population. By their sheer voting power the tribesmen today rule the country. The pressure on the

Creoles has been rapidly building up and their privileged position
has been seriously threatened.

In the face of this mounting pressure, the Creoles tried to organise
themselves formally within an all-Creole party. But the majority of
the Creoles soon realised that such a step would be suicidal because,
being numerically weak, they would not be able to secure any
effective representation in parliament. What is more, the non-
Creoles might decide to allot jobs, scholarships and other benefits
to the Creoles in proportion to their numbers and that would be
disastrous in its consequences.

It was during this period of mounting threats and frustrations that
more and more Creole men joined the Freemasonic order. The
number of lodges thus increased from six in 1947 to seventeen in
1970. This increase did not occur gradually but in two dramatic
jumps, in 1947–52 and in 1965–8. What is common to both periods
is that each involved new, serious threats to Creole power. The
same men whose power was threatened were the men who joined
the fraternity, and unless we assume that these men were split
personalities it is evident that the two processes were interconnected.

This does not in any way mean that the men joined the fraternity
to protect their privileges. Men join for a variety of individual
reasons. Indeed, many find intrinsic values in the beliefs, rituals
and ceremonies of the order. What is more, the Freemasonic
movement is officially opposed to the discussion of politics in the
course of its meetings. There is certainly no conscious and deliberate
use of Freemasonry in political manoeuvring. But all this does not
mean that the order is of no political significance.

Without any deliberate policy, Freemasonic rituals and activities
became mechanisms for the articulation of an informal organisation,
which helped the Creoles to co-ordinate their corporate efforts in
the face of mounting pressures and threats. Although the members
are distributed among seventeen lodges under two separate con-
stitutions, they are very closely interrelated through multiple lodge
affiliation. A man can become a member in only one lodge, but
can be affiliated to other lodges within his own or the other con-
stitution. Some Creoles are affiliated within as many as five different
lodges. More interaction between the different lodges takes place
in the form of intervisiting. At any lodge meeting there can be
scores of visitors from other lodges. What is sociologically significant in lodge activities is not the formal rituals of the order but

the banqueting following these rituals. Here, amidst heavy drinking and eating, the members engage in the process of true 'fraternising'. This informal institution within masonry is perhaps the most fundamental mechanism in welding the members of all the lodges into a single organisation, with numerous channels of communication between them.

But the most important contribution of Freemasonic organisation to informal Creole organisation is in the development of a unified authority structure and leadership. During the colonial period, while the Temne, Mende and the other tribes of Sierra Leone had their own local and paramount chiefs whose authority was upheld by the Colonial administration, the Creoles were without a unified traditional leadership. The difficulty in developing a unified leadership and a system of authority was further increased by the fact that, outside the formal political arena, the Creoles had several different groupings, like the church, and the different occupational groupings. Furthermore, there was intensive strife within each grouping characterised by intense competition for promotion into higher positions and by perpetual tension between superior and subordinate within the bureaucratic structure. But when the members of these groupings became incorporated within the Masonic lodges, they became integrated within an all encompassing authority structure in which members from the higher positions of the different non-Masonic hierarchies were included. The different types and bases of power within those groupings were expressed in terms of the uniform symbols and ideology of Freemasonry (for a more detailed account of this case see Cohen 1971).

Within Sierra Leone, the Creoles were not unique in using a secret society for organisational articulation. The Mende and other tribes have their own traditional secret societies which they frequently use in modern political settings. The Mende used their secret society, the Poro, to organise and stage an uprising against the British in 1898 and have since been using the symbols, ideology and organisation of the society to mobilise votes and support in elections (see Little 1965; 1966; Kilson 1967).

Almost everywhere in the world different types of secret ritual groupings are manipulated in the articulation of organisational functions for a variety of political purposes. In its history in Europe, Freemasonry has itself served to organise conservative as well as progressive movements.

But the role of secrecy is not confined to organised groupings. As Simmel (1950:334) points out, every human relation is characterised, among other things, by the amount of secrecy that is in and around it. Indeed, all that Marx called 'mystification' involves a large element of concealment. The more privileged a group is in society, the more secretive and mystifying it tends to be about its organisation and strategies. This does not mean that members of these groups consciously and deliberately use the symbolism of concealment and mystification in a brazen, utilitarian manner. Often what might have been at first a symbolic performance staged to mystify outsiders is unconsciously adopted by the performers as an end in itself, convincing themselves, as much as the outsiders, of the validity of their symbolic formations and ideology.

Cousinhoods

One of the institutions linking an élite, like that of the City of London, together is intermarriage. It is, however, difficult to assess the contribution of marriage to the informal organisation of this élite because there are other symbolic forms operating in its organisation at the same time, like patterns of friendships. The difficulty is increased by the fact that this élite is methodologically difficult to delineate and to study. Indeed, as Sampson points out (1962:345), it was only thanks to the Bank Rate Tribunal of 1957 and the Radcliffe Report of 1959 that anything is known about the mysterious ways in which the City operates, and about the men who are involved in it. But it is possible to find cases that are methodologically easier to study.

One such case is provided by Bermant in a book, *The Cousinhood: The Anglo-Jewish Gentry* (1971). This is a detailed and extensively documented study of a number of wealthy Anglo-Jewish families who became intensively interrelated with one another through marriages in successive generations and eventually were transformed into an exclusive group whose men became related to one another as cousins. The material that Bermant presents is adequate enough to make it possible to consider the cousinhood developmentally, over a period of about 150 years, and to see this development in relation to political and economic changes in the wider British society.

The cousinhood began to form early in the nineteenth century when these wealthy families – Cohens, Rothschilds, Montefiores, Samuels, Goldsmids, Franklins, Montagus, Waleys, Henriques, and later Sassoons – began to intermarry. They were Jews who strongly felt the effects of the civic disabilities from which Jews in Britain suffered at the time. Jews could not be called to the Bar, were not accepted in the ancient universities of Cambridge and Oxford, could not be elected to parliament or to municipal councils. Even on the Stock Exchange they were limited to twelve seats. The families therefore joined together to co-ordinate their efforts to try to end these disabilities.

It is difficult to specify one single factor leading to the formation of the cousinhood. The families involved were Jewish and could not at the time marry outside their religious group. They were also wealthy and high in status and could not marry down within Judaism. Even without the civic disabilities they would probably have intermarried homogamously in order to keep status, protect wealth and co-operate in business. And because of their wealth and status, it was they, more than the other Jews in Britain – most of these were at that time destitute, living on the donations of the wealthy – who felt the frustrations caused by those disabilities. It was thus a combination of these factors that brought about the formation of the cousinhood. As men in one generation intermarried and became related as affines, their sons and daughters became related as cousins in the next generation. As Bermant puts it, fortune was married to fortune, with blood and money circulating within the same small group. Bermant documents these linkages and cross-linkages in extensive genealogical charts.

Thus by the middle of the nineteenth century, the cousinhood emerges from the records as an exclusive, distinct, though informally organised, interest group in which there was a unique concentration of wealth, political connections and influence. The members were distinct as Jews from non-Jews and as 'cousins' from the rest of the Jews. The close-knit network of patrilateral, matrilateral and affinal relationships linking its members served as effective means of communication, deliberation, decision-making, and co-ordination of political action.

Their efforts bore fruit and during the second half of the century all the disabilities were removed. In the process, the cousinhood amassed more and more wealth, with many of their branches becoming landed gentry. It was only in recent decades that the group began to disintegrate, as a result of political emancipation and consequently of increasing assimilation within the wider British society. In other words, the structural conditions that brought the cousinhood into being disappeared.

The symbolism of kinship was effective in articulating a great deal of the organisational functions of this interest group because the group was relatively small. In larger groups, the web of kinship resulting from the practice of endogamy can only serve as an auxiliary symbolic form combining with other forms to articulate the major organisational functions. (The effects of increasing size on such groups is discussed in detail in Cohen 1972.) In some cases it may become a principal mechanism for the solution of one major organisational function. This can be seen in another cousinhood which I myself studied.

I am referring here to the Creoles of Sierra Leone whom I discussed in the previous section. The Creoles of Freetown, who number about 27,000, are highly endogamous. They are bilateral in their kinship organisation, without any emphasis on either patrilineal or matrilineal descent. Relationships are traced in both lines and property passes according to British civil law, without favouring one line over the other. Men freely decide on whether to adopt the family name of their father, or of their mother, usually depending on which of the two names is associated with higher prestige. In some cases both names are adopted by a man, linking them with a hyphen. On marriage, women adopt their husband's family name, or retain their father's or mother's family name, or hyphenate the family name of one of their parents with that of the husband.

It is evident from this that in these circumstances it is almost impossible to give any clear boundary to define the people you call 'my family'. Even if you go up to only three generations in the genealogy of a man in both lines, the number of relatives will be very great. And if you take account of all the other links then the persons you include within your 'family' will be so vast that it will practically be co-extensive with the whole of Creoldom. It is indeed no exaggeration to say that any Creole can trace a kinship relationship to any other Creole man. Mention a name of a Creole to another Creole and you are bound to be told: 'He is my cousin' – particularly if the name you mention is of an important man.

It is also evident that the group of persons you call your 'family' is different from that which your brother or your cousin calls his 'family'. One's family is an egocentric entity. Nevertheless, a degree of permanence and discreteness is given to a set of kin through the system of patronage. Each important man serves as the patron of a large number of kinsmen some of whom will even adopt his name, whether they are related to him patrilaterally, matrilaterally or affinally. A 'family' of this type includes both patron and client. Although there is a strong tendency for the wealthy and eminent to seek close social relations with their equals in status, there are strong economic, political, moral and ritual forces that link the members together.

The picture which emerges is thus that of a few hundred important men, each heading a large 'family' of a few scores of kinsmen and affines who emphasise their link to him. The relationships that hold such a grouping together are moral relationships and are governed by categorical values and norms. A Creole will genuinely abhor any suggestion that these relationships are instrumental as means to material ends. But this does not mean that they are not, nevertheless, also utilitarian.

Sierra Leone is still a developing country, where there inevitably are a great deal of difficulties in the administrative process. As in all developing countries, the bureaucracy is slow and irregular and at times the conditions for the maintenance of law and order are not fully prevalent. For a group like the Creoles, who own property, need educational services and jobs, seek promotion and travel extensively, their demands on, and need for, the bureaucracy are extensive. In these circumstances, the most effective way of operating is through personal contacts. Among the Creoles all is done through the network of 'cousins'. The large extended 'families' are endlessly linked and cross-linked through the simultaneous multiple family memberships of their respective members. The result is that any man within any 'family' can find a channel to any important man in any other family for help and support. Creoldom can thus be seen in this respect to be a vast cousinhood whose structure is validated and maintained by a variety of extensive ceremonials and of other forms of symbolic formations and activities.

As the Creoles are a minority and are under constant political pressure, it is imperative that the wealthy and powerful should help the less wealthy and powerful among them. The Jewish cousinhood in Britain in the nineteenth century did the same with poorer Jews.

But while the Jewish cousinhood acted corporately as patrons for the rest of the Jews, the Creoles 'distribute' their poorer strata among the patrons. In both cases the obligation to help was maintained and validated in terms of ritual symbols. In the case of the Jews, it was the religious Judaic values and practices; among the Creoles it was the mystical values and rituals connected with the dead.

Cousinhoods, like those of the Anglo-Jews and the Creoles, can be developed and maintained mainly by marrying all or most of the women of the group within the group. The men thus become related to one another as cousins through the females of the group. As this pattern of marriage is consistently followed, an 'alliance' is established. The group becomes distinct, exclusive, closely knit. In the process, the females of the group become a vested interest for the men. In these circumstances it becomes necessary for the men to control, somehow, the movement of their sisters and daughters in marriage. Mechanisms are developed by which the women of the group are coerced or, as often is the case, indirectly persuaded to marry within the group, and discouraged from marrying outside the group.

These features of organisational articulation through the exchange of women can be discussed in the course of examining the structure of a third type of cousinhood, that of Arab villagers in the Middle East. I shall make use of my own study of Arab villages in Israel, along the border with Jordan.

The Arab village consists of a few groups which, for brevity, I shall describe as lineages. The lineages vary in size. In the area where I worked, a lineage was a few hundred strong. Under the political circumstances prevailing at the time of field work, the lineage played fundamental political roles (for details see Cohen 1965). The Arab lineage is organised on the myth of patrilineal descent, with the members claiming descent from a common ancestor. The claim is validated by a detailed genealogy.

But the sheer cognitive belief in common descent is not by itself a sufficient mechanism for keeping the group together. In many systems the principle of descent is objectified, upheld and kept alive by patterns of ritual beliefs and practices. For example, among the Lugbara (Middleton 1960), the Chinese (Freedman 1958; 1966) and the Tallensi of Ghana (Fortes 1945) the myth of patriliny is supported by elaborate cults of ancestor worship. In other words, the men of such a lineage are in effect held together through sharing the mystical beliefs and practices involved in this cult. Among the Arabs, however, no such cult exists. Instead, the group is held together through an elaborate body of symbolic beliefs and practices related to the women of the group. In effect, the Arab patrilineage consists of men who are intensively linked together through their marriage to one another's sisters or daughters. Those lineages that practise ancestor worship are usually exogamous, with men being forced, through the beliefs and sanctions of incest, to give their women to other lineages in exchange for wives from those other lineages. The Arab patrilineage on the other hand upholds the norms of parallel-cousin marriage. Men have the right to claim in marriage women from the group.

The Arab lineage is not totally endogamous. The ratio of in-lineage marriage varies from group to group. Generally, the wealthier and more powerful a group is the higher the ratio of in-lineage marriage. Some lineages in the area maintain a strict prohibition on giving any women to outsiders. Many others, however, give half of their women to outsiders and marry the other half inside. But even if the lineage is not totally endogamous, the substantial proportion of the internal marriages is sufficient to link its members intensely and, to some extent, mark the group off from other groups in this respect. Thus, in one specific lineage with a relatively low ratio of in-group marriage, 34 out of a total of 72 marriages were contracted within the group (which numbered 314 people) while 25 marriages were contracted with women from the rest of the village (with a population of about 2,000 people) and another 13 marriages with women from many villages in the area, within a population totalling many thousands. While relationships created by the 38 marriages contracted outside the group are with people who are scattered among a large population, the relationships formed by the 34 marriages within the relatively small lineage are sufficient to create a closely knit network which links the various families of the group together. These relationships within the lineage are intense and complex because they overlap and also cut across one another. The same men are linked together in a variety of ways which impose on them a variety of obligations towards one another.

Thus the political unity of the lineage, which formally hinges on the principle of unilineal descent, is made possible by these in-group marriages. There is a close correlation between the ratio of in-lineage marriage and the unity of the lineage as it manifests itself in actual political action. The villagers themselves often explain their preference for in-group marriage in political terms. They say that children born of such marriages experience no divided loyalties because they have the same men as their father's brothers and mother's brothers, and their loyalties therefore 'remain within their camp'. In lineages with exogamous systems men are often inhibited from resort to violence against other lineages to which their sisters and daughters are married.

The females of the lineage are a means for the unity of the lineage in yet another, interconnected, respect. These Arab villages, like many other Mediterranean communities, observe a most elaborate and complicated code system in relation to the honour of women. The most crucial criterion of prestige is the intensity of the jealousy that men publicly demonstrate in guarding the honour of their sisters and daughters. An adulterous woman, even an unmarried woman having a sexual affair with a man, must be killed by her brothers or her father's brothers' sons. If she is killed, the group not only reasserts its position but also rises in the prestige scale. If she is not killed, they suffer a great loss of prestige. This constitutes an additional reason why lineages prefer to marry their women within. For it is the lineage as a political group which is responsible for the protection of the honour of its women. The men of a lineage are thus linked together through both rights and obligations in relation to one another's sisters and daughters. They are further linked as affines and as matrilateral kin.

Because of this fundamental function of the females of the group in holding the group together, the marriage of the women of the group is decided upon by the political leadership of the lineage. A man who is asked the hand of his daughter in marriage by outsiders will say 'I will consult and let you know' or 'ask her hand from her paternal uncles'. In the evening he would go to the central guest house of the lineage and inform the leaders about it. They begin first to enquire why no man from within the lineage would marry the girl. But even if no lineage man is available to marry her the elders may decide to veto the proposed marriage.

Marriage is thus very much involved in politics within the village. The arrangement of marriage involves political manoeuvring on the village level and there is hardly a political dispute or alliance which does not involve in one way or another a number of marriages. Often purely domestic issues between spouses and their immediate kin cause political repercussions involving political groupings. The stability of marriage is intimately interconnected with political factors and surveys show that an in-lineage marriage is twice as stable as an out-of-lineage marriage.

It is obvious that in these circumstances everything is done to ensure that women abide by the decisions of the lineage about their marriage. This is why women are insulated from men through the institution of seclusion. Men of the lineage are further armed by the injunction of Islamic family law which regards women as legal minors. A woman cannot marry herself off to a man. She can be given off in marriage to a man only by another man – her father, brother, or kinsman.

Thus, whenever men form alliances through the exchange of women, mechanisms are developed to ensure the compliance of women. In the caste system this is achieved through rigid ritual rules. In American and other western societies it is done through subtle symbolic mechanisms. Opportunities are created for women to meet and date men 'from the right circles'. In the American mixed massive university campuses the sororities and fraternities take care of this. Further, women are trained through socialisation that their status is derived from the status of the man they marry. A woman will thus be inhibited by various social constraints from marrying below the class of her father and brothers. Most women will therefore end up marrying within their status group and thereby indirectly achieve significant organisational functions. To conclude, the Jewish, Creole and Arab cousinhoods achieved a good deal of their distinctiveness through a high proportion of in-group marriage. As endogamy is continued over many generations the collectivity is transformed into a 'descent group', with descent being defined either in terms of patrilineality, as in the Arab case, or of bilaterality, as in the other two cases. In all three cases, the network of patrilateral, matrilateral and affinal relationships that are created and recreated by endogamy have served as channels for communication, and the values, norms and beliefs that govern them have helped in evolving an informal authority structure and mechanisms for decision-making. The role of endogamy in the articulation of group ideology was clearly seen in the case of the

Arab lineage whose men are held together by, among other links, the complex code of 'honour and shame' associated with the women of the group. Finally, the role of endogamy in group socialisation was in the extensive, elaborate, and costly 'family ceremonials' of the Creoles.

The contribution of endogamy to the different organisational functions of a group is, however, affected by the size of the group. Other things remaining the same, an increase in the size of the group will bring about a weakening in the channels of communication, the structure of authority and in decision-making procedures. A group of, say, 100 men will be more intimately linked by the *same ratio* of in-group marriage than a group of 1,000. The Arab lineage tends to divide as a result of increasing size mainly because of weakening authority and decision-making mechanisms. When a group becomes as large as the Creoles in Sierra Leone without being able to divide, endogamy will have to be combined with other articulating symbolic forms to make up for weaknesses created by size. Thus, as indicated earlier, the Creoles became intensely freemasonised when they needed a unified authority structure and decision-making procedures. On the other hand, an increase in the size of the group will not affect the contribution of endogamy to distinctiveness, ideology and socialisation. The 'rape complex' is as powerful in rallying a large group, like the Whites in Rhodesia or South Africa, as in rallying a small group like the Arab lineage. Indeed the ideology of sex is an integral part of the political system in such large-scale societies as those of South Africa, Rhodesia and traditional India.

Conclusions: symbolic action in the politics of stratification

Stratification in two dimensions
The 'lineage' of complex society
The lesson of political science
The demystification of hierarchy
The crucial politico-symbolic drama
The relevance of 'mumbo-jumbology'

The few case studies discussed in the previous chapter indicate how, in a variety of circumstances, economico-political groupings that cannot organise themselves in formal associations adopt a variety of symbolic strategies to co-ordinate their corporate activities. The cases should not be seen as different, mutually exclusive types of groupings. Most informally organised interest groups make use of the same symbolic forms to articulate the same symbolic functions, though circumstances inevitably create a measure of uniqueness in each case. The different symbolic forms, like religion and kinship, are differently emphasised in different groups with some groups making more use of one form than of other forms. The forms are differently combined in different groups. Furthermore, as groups sometimes overlap, sectional groups exploit different forms from those utilised by the wider, more inclusive, groups. Thus the Jewish cousinhood utilised kinship and marriage to set themselves apart from the more inclusive grouping of British Jews who exploited religion as an articulating principle. Other groups, like the Creoles of Sierra Leone, exploit, in an almost equal measure, a number of forms at one and the same time: descent, marriage, cousinhood, religion, secret rituals, cult of the dead, style of life. Fundamentally all these groups are structurally the same. They are all interest groups, protecting or developing power for their members through informal organisational mechanisms. The particular cases have been selected and treated in a way that makes it possible to highlight the significance of one institution, or symbolic form, at a time.

Stratification in two dimensions

In discussing informally organised interest groups of this type we are in effect dealing with some of the fundamental issues concerning the analysis of social stratification generally.

The study of social stratification has been one of the major preoccupations of modern sociology. One need not be a Marxian in order to realise that the distribution of wealth, power and prestige is the key to the understanding of a multitude of socio-cultural phenomena in our massive, complex, industrial society. There is therefore a vast sociological literature on this subject. This literature is varied in terms of the problems investigated, the levels of social organisation considered, the number of variables covered in the analysis, and in terms of the methods used. This variation makes it difficult to generalise about the nature and achievements of this endeavour.

Nevertheless, it will not be a great distortion of the facts to state that the analysis of stratification, both in the USA and in western Europe, has been dominated by the formulations of Weber. Just as Weber was said to have been arguing with the shadow of Marx, so has the main body of sociology in these countries been reacting to the theoretical problems delineated by Weber's three-dimensional scale of stratification. This in itself can be a healthy sign. As sociology has so often been criticised for being 'non-cumulative', concentration on a limited number of related problems that are explored within the same methodological and theoretical framework can lead to the development of a body of interrelated hypotheses and the cumulation of findings.

But what has actually happened is that one sociologist after another has produced more and more abstract, national-level, highly-conjectural formulations whose sociological value has been very limited. One of the main reasons for this limitation of our research endeavour has been the continued preoccupation with large-scale stratification systems. Inevitably, this has led to the construction of conceptual class categories ranked in one order or another. With the aid of national surveys and censuses, scholars have constructed more and more 'strata'. This, again, can be an important contribution to the study of stratification, but only if it led to the development of further research, by breaking the major analytical problems into strategically smaller ones and subjecting these to further empirical and verifiable research. But the hold of the macro-structural construction on some students of society is such that even when researchers concentrate on the study of small local communities, they often attempt to discover the existence of the national strata in the local ones. Many sociologists seem to give the primacy of existence to classes, not to the groupings that make them.

Little advance can be made in the study of the distribution of power in industrial society unless we begin to operate systematically in terms of specific interest groups, their scope, organisation and interrelationships. Even students of the caste system of India have come now to the same realisation. 'The real unit of the caste system', writes Srinivas (1952), 'is not one of the five *varnas* but *jati*, which is a very small endogamous group practising a traditional occupation and enjoying a certain amount of the cultural, ritual and juridical autonomy.' The detailed study of such local caste groups by some anthropologists and sociologists has greatly shaken our views about the rigidity and stability of the caste system. As Srinivas points out, the caste system is far from being a rigid structure (271) and disputes are one of its essential features (266). If this is the case with the Indian system, it should be far more so with western-type systems. India is a country with an under-developed economy and its social system has been governed by a unitary, predominant ideology with many centuries of stability and consolidation behind it. In the West, on the other hand, the economy is highly diversified, society is differentiated and complex, change is rapid and dynamic, and different cultures, with different symbolic codes, and different ideologies and cults, compete with one another. Under these conditions, the units of our study should be middle-range power groups, not the transcending, vaguely conceived class categories. The political scientist's conception of society as being pluralistic, in the sense of consisting of various types of interest, or power, groups which quarrel, compete, co-operate and federate in a continuous attempt to defend achieved positions of privilege, or to obtain more privileges – this picture is heuristically more promising as a research strategy in the study of the distribution of power and prestige in industrial society than the ordinary survey method. Even in a hierarchical system like that of India where one ideology is presumed to articulate the whole system, it will be possible to see which interest group or groups impose that ideology on the other groups and for what purpose. Similarly, even if we accept the Marxian doctrine that the class structure tends to be articulated in terms of the mystifications of the ruling class, those mystifications can be studied as the strategy and ideology of an interest group *vis-à-vis* the other groups in society.

To elaborate on this point further, a second reason for the limitations in our sociological literature on stratification should be pointed out. I am referring here to Weber's three dimensions of stratification: 'class, status and party'. The differentiation between class and politics in this model is maintained only by adopting a narrow definition of power and politics. Power is defined in terms of the politics of the state, and it has been easy for sociologists to point out many cases of 'incongruities' between economic power and political power. For instance, it is pointed out that some groups can be wealthy but without any share in the politics of the state. Heuristically, this distinction is not only of little analytical value, but can be misleading. Power is an aspect of all social relationships and is not limited to the politics of the state. Political authority is composite in its structure, being maintained by different types of social power. Economic power is an integral part of political power. As Dahrendorf (1968) points out, economic inequality exists because there is law. A wealthy minority may have no direct representation in the central government but can exercise a great deal of power which can indirectly affect government policy. Indeed, Packard (1961) goes so far as to state that in modern America you can exert power only by denying you have it and some political scientists have revealed to our view 'anonymous empires', a multiplicity of interest groups that greatly affect politics without formally participating in government.

The restricted definition of politics has also thwarted the advance of the analysis of interest groups by political scientists. These generally refrain from describing and treating interest groups as political. Thus Holtzman (1966:11) states that 'interest groups become political only when they endeavour to work through or upon government'. (For similar statements see also Finer 1958; Hunt 1956; Castles 1967.) The contention by some sociologists and political scientists that if we adopted an extensive definition of politics we would not be able to develop its study because it would then be coterminous with all social relations, is based on a descriptive, not an analytical, orientation. It is always possible to work with sets of social relations at a time, such as those implicit in interest groups. Interest groups represent concentrations of power and are thus the very stuff of which politics generally is made. Thus, if we are to advance our study of the distribution of power, we must reduce the dimensions of our model to two: power and the symbolism of status.

The second limitation imposed by the Weberian model is the narrow conception of status. Briefly, status according to many sociologists is 'expressive', psychological. In a stable on-going system it is an epiphenomenon of class, though it dies hard, as it continues for long after the economic base is gone.

But even if status is originally expressive, this does not preclude it from being, at the same time, instrumental. As I indicated earlier, the symbolic patterns of behaviour that are implicit in the special style of life of a status group performs, though informally, many organisational functions, like distinctiveness, communication and authority. There is thus an intimate interdependence between formal and informal mechanisms for the articulation of the organisation of a power group. When an organisational function cannot be articulated formally, informal mechanisms are adopted. As our society is officially egalitarian, in the sense that classes are not formally recognised, and as it is not possible for a class to organise itself as such on formal lines, 'class groups' make extensive use of their patterns of symbolic behaviour to organise themselves.

The 'lineage' of complex society

If we operate in terms of power groups, instead of classes, we shall be able to solve such theoretical problems as those posed by cases of 'incongruity' between status and power. One of the classic crucial cases often cited by students of stratification is that a worker may get the same income as that of a man with middle-class status and yet the two men will not be of the same status. They will continue to have different styles of life derived from their respective status groups. What we must look for here is not just the amount of income that the men get but also the source of this income and the prospects for the future. In situations such as this one, it is often better to be a poor man associated with wealthier men than to be a poor man associated with poor men. A low income man within a high status group has possibilities through his links with men from the same status group in such matters as promotion, better appointments, better education for his children, better marriage arrangements. On the other hand, a man from what you may rate as an upper working-class group will probably stick to the group which has enabled him to achieve his present income and status. Informally organised interest groups need not be homogeneous in the class of their members. To be a member of an informally organised interest group you need not only adopt the style of life of that group but also to be hooked onto the dense network of interpersonal relationships between the members of the group. In Sierra Leone it is possible for a non-Creole to dress, worship, behave, eat, etc., like a Creole but he will not partake of the privileges of being a Creole unless he succeeds in grafting himself onto the Creole cousinhood network. If we avoid analysis in terms of hypothetical horizontal strata and operate in terms of interest groups it will be possible, without any contradictions, to conceive of differential distribution of power within the group itself.

In my view, the study of the structure of the informally organised interest group is a key to the development of an anthropology of complex society. Complexity as Mitchell (1966:41) points out can be unravelled by the development of simple formulations. Segmentary society was complex until the idea of the 'lineage' became available. Thus, a Nuer local settlement would certainly present a chaotic picture of people hailing from different clans, one of which is dominant while the others are not. The men belong to different age-sets and have their political loyalties with men living in other localities. Men from the same clan are forced by the rules of exogamy to marry women from other clans. Brothers are forced to marry wives from different clans. A man must have children to perpetuate his name. If he dies without having had children his family would marry a woman to his name and one of the brothers of the deceased man would co-habit with the woman but the children conceived in this way would bear the name of the deceased man. Widows are inherited by the brothers or patrilineal cousins of the deceased husbands. Women can legally marry women. Thus, the settlement would certainly present a bewildering situation in which it would be difficult for an outsider to find out which woman belongs to which man and which child to which parent. The networks of patrilateral, matrilateral and affinal relationships created in this way will indeed be very complex. But all of this 'anarchy' gives way to understandable order when the lineage system, which provides the 'bony structure' of the society, is delineated. (For details see Evans-Pritchard 1940a; 1951a.)

Similarly, a residential quarter in a modern city would present a complex picture of men and women hailing from different localities, working in different parts of the city, belonging to different occupational, political, religious and cultural associations. Even in African cities, only few quarters are inhabited by culturally homogeneous populations as is the case with the Hausa community in Ibadan discussed in the last chapter. In most cases, localities are but dormitories for people who work and interact socially in other parts of the city. With present-day means of transport and of communication the residential area is no longer significant for social interaction. Creole families in the residentially mixed quarters of Freetown often take their children in their cars to play with 'the right kind' of children in other parts of the city.

The 'lineages' of modern society are the interest groups which compete, quarrel and co-operate in the struggle for power and privilege. They range in organisation from the most formal at one end to the most informal at the other. Anthropology specialises in the identification and analysis of groups nearer to the informal end of the continuum. The concept of the informally organised group, in its two dimensions, its functions, development, structure and the variety of cultural forms, can clarify a whole array of sociocultural phenomena in contemporary complex society. It can be an important methodological tool in both field work and in analysis.

The lesson of political science

But, to make the right use of this concept, the political anthropologist will have to learn an elementary lesson from political science. The small areas of social life, in whose study social anthropology specialises, are now everywhere becoming integral parts of large-scale social systems. Micro-sociological techniques cannot by themselves deal with the higher levels of these systems. Social anthropologists have been well aware of this problem and to deal with it have developed such concepts as 'social field' and 'plural society'. These are purely descriptive concepts and the question is not whether they are valid or not but whether they are helpful in analysis. They are certainly helpful in directing our attention to certain characteristics of the new societies but, in my view, they do not face the central problem squarely. One of the most important developments of our time is the emergence of the new states of the 'Third World'. In both the developing and the developed societies, the state is today the greatest holder and arbiter of economic and political power.

Social anthropologists have done a great deal of work on relatively small-scale primitive states. But, apart from a few exceptions (see, for example, Lloyd 1955; Bailey 1960, 1963; Mayer 1962; Cohen 1965) they have ignored the importance of the modern state in the study of the politics of small communities, for two main reasons. The first is that when they initially became aware of this problem, many of the communities which they studied were in lands still under colonial rule. This was particularly the case in Africa, where international boundaries had been largely the creation of colonial powers. In former British territories, indirect rule helped to perpetuate the exclusiveness and autonomy of the relatively small tribal communities. In those circumstances there was no 'state' to consider and the most that an anthropologist could do was to try to study the colonial administration. But although some anthropologists began over thirty years ago to advocate that the European administrator and missionary should be studied along with the native chief and witch doctor as part of the same political system (see Schapera 1938), no serious attempts were made to probe into the domain of the colonial administration. One reason was that in some cases it was the colonial government which initiated and financed the research. In many other cases the anthropologist tended to emphasise traditional socio-cultural systems and to minimise the significance of change brought about by modern conditions.

The second main reason why anthropologists have not taken the modern state as the context within which the analysis of small communities should be made, is their earlier objections to the study of political philosophy which had dominated the study of the state until about the time of the Second World War. The tone was set by the editors of *African Political Systems* when they stated that they had found the theories of political philosophers to be of little scientific value because their conclusions were not formulated in terms of observed behaviour (Fortes and Evans-Pritchard 1940:4).

This last objection is no longer relevant because the state is now being *empirically* studied by political science which has grown in stature in the last two decades. In the USA and Britain alone, enormous financial and manpower resources have been allocated to the empirical study of state-level politics in both the developed and developing countries. There has been a spectacular proliferation of departments of political science in the universities, with corresponding facilities for research, travel and publication (see Wiseman 1967; Mackenzie 1967; SSRC 1968). Some excellent monographs and articles on the politics of countries of the Third World have been published and are being used in courses in political science in the universities.

While it is true that political science is still 'looking for its identity' (Easton 1968) and that it is still exploring various approaches that have become the specialisations of different schools of thought within it, there is, nevertheless, an underlying orientation towards the study of state-level phenomena, and it is in this respect that political anthropologists can learn a great deal.

Some anthropologists may dismiss the findings of political science for this very reason, i.e. for political science being 'macro-political'. They would argue that it takes an anthropologist over a year of field work, and many years of processing and analysing his data, to make a study of the social system of a simple community of a few hundred people; and that it is therefore absurd to attach any scientific value to the findings of political scientists who make generalisations about whole societies with many millions of inhabitants. But this argument ignores two fundamental issues. The first is that because the state exists and plays such a crucial role in changing the structure and the culture of our small communities, someone must study it. Such a study is essential not only academically but also for a variety of practical, mainly administrative, considerations. It is absurd to say that the study of the state, as a whole, should await the development of 'micro-sociology'; this may be a long-term development and, in the meantime, the political scientist is meeting the challenge. The second is that political science has developed new concepts and new techniques for dealing with state-level political phenomena in an effective way. There has been a revolution in methods of indexing vast amounts of information, processing them and employing them in future analysis (see Mackenzie 1967:66-74; Deutsch 1966).

Political science today approaches the study of small communities and groups with reference to the state. In the political scientists' conceptual framework, the tribes, bands and isolated communities, which have been the major object of anthropological studies, are now either in the process of integration within new socio-cultural entities or, if for any political reasons they still cling to their traditional identity, the most that can be said about their distinctiveness is that they are 'interest groups' exerting pressure on the state or on groups within the state. Thus, as I indicated in the last chapter, the phenomenon called 'tribalism' or 'retribalisation' in contemporary African societies is the result, not of ethnic groups disengaging themselves from one another after independence, but of increasing interaction between them, within the context of new political situations. It is the outcome, not of conservatism, but of a dynamic socio-cultural change which is brought about by new cleavages and new alignments of power within the framework of the new state.

A great deal of progress in the study of such 'interest groups' has been made in recent years by political scientists. Indeed, many political scientists see the political structure of the state as being 'pluralistic' – using this term in a different sense from that of social anthropologists – that is, as consisting of innumerable groupings of various sorts which mediate between the individual and the state (see Bentley 1949; Finer 1958; Eckstein 1960). The development of interest groups, and the nature of the relationships between them and the state, depends to some extent on the structure of

CONCLUSION

the state. Some states allow a great deal of group 'pluralism';
other states discourage or even prevent the development of such
groupings by conducting an endless struggle against them. These
differences between states have been studied by political scientists
empirically and comparatively (see Ehrmann 1964; Castles 1967).
The term 'political culture' has been sometimes used to describe
these structural differences between states. The anthropologist who
studies small groups within the contemporary state cannot afford
to ignore such studies. Indeed, I go further and say that the
anthropologist must *deliberately* formulate his problems in such a
way as to make reference to the state a necessary part of his analysis.

The demystification of hierarchy

The informally organised interest groups which we seek to study
are no longer discrete and easily identifiable collectivities. The
members of such a group are often residentially dispersed. They
may have different occupations in different localities. They carry
no formal emblems to signify their group identity. Indeed, their
grouping may often be 'camouflaged' and sometimes 'invisible'.
The greater the power and privilege they share, the more exclusive
they become.

Exclusiveness tends inevitably to create an atmosphere of secrecy.
Sometimes this secrecy is an established formal principle such as
that of the Freemasonic order, or of some student fraternities and
sororities in the USA. But more often, even without any such
formal policy, secrecy surrounds exclusive gatherings and organisations. This air of secrecy is an essential component of the art of
what Marx called 'mystification' which is found in hierarchical
systems. As Keller (1968:3) remarks:

> The existence and persistence of influential minorities is one of the
> constant characteristics of organized social life. . . . Like a secret society,
> those at the top rarely reveal the inner workings of their worlds.

Simmel (1950:345) points out that: 'The purpose of secrecy is
above all, *protection*. Of all protective measures, the most radical
is to make oneself invisible.' I believe that because the style of life
of élite groups is instrumental in their effective organisation and
survival, these groups tend to cling to the principle of 'privacy' in
order not to give away their organisational strategies or to unmask

their mystifications. This is the main reason why so little study has been possible of groups from middle and higher 'classes' in countries such as Britain and the USA, to say nothing of totalitarian countries. This contrasts sharply with the abundance of studies of groups from working 'classes'. Working 'classes' have nothing to lose by revealing the patterns of their way of life. The more privileged groups, on the other hand, can lose a great deal. In their domination of the Hutu in Ruanda (Maquet 1961), the Tutsi claimed that they were themselves a different type of human beings which made them naturally superior to the Hutu, that among other things, they lived on liquids, mainly milk, and ate no solid foods. To maintain the myth, the Tutsi had to swear their Hutu servants to secrecy, as these saw their masters actually eating solid foods in the privacy of their homes.

The identification and delineation of 'invisible' interest groups in modern society can be sociologically as significant as the analysis of their structure. In this task of identification the researcher is forced to rely on two main clumsy 'crutches' of enquiry. The first is the observation of visible patterns of symbolic action and formations. The theoretical assumption here is that if symbols are live and significant it is because they are carried by a collectivity of people. The question will then arise of who these people are and what interests they share together. The second 'crutch' is to start from the other end and to try to identify interests and the men who are behind them. The assumption here is that if the interests are significant, then the group must develop basic organisational mechanisms to co-ordinate the members' activities in the development, protection and maintenance of these interests. The researcher will often shift from the one front to the other, seizing on a clue here to use it for further discovery there and then, with more clues back here, and so on.

To illuminate the methodological problems in such situations, we can consider cases of groups that are in the process of 'going invisible'. Many of the cases discussed in the last chapter can be relevant here. The process is clearly seen among the Creoles of Sierra Leone (see above, pp. 107-10 and pp. 112-18). With the rise of the natives to political power after independence, it became clear to the Creoles that, because of their numerical weakness, it would be disastrous for their highly privileged position to cling to their ethnic distinctiveness. They began to play down their traditional identity, pointing out that 'tribalism' was a remnant of the colonial period and that they were all Sierra Leoneans. Many of them today emphasise family connections with the natives. Some of the men have even changed their British names to African names, and many others now give their children African (usually Yoruba or Muslim) names. The Creoles are fast 'passing out of Creoldom' and it is possible that in one or two generations they will have abandoned many of the well-known symbols of their distinctiveness. But the group is still there and the old symbols of distinctiveness are being replaced by new ones in an on-going process of cultural metamorphosis.

In the process of identifying an 'invisible' group organisation, two holistic pictures will emerge. The one of the network of power relationships of its members both inside and outside the group. The other of the patterns of symbolic formations that are carried by the group. The analysis of the dialectical interdependence between these two features of the group can then proceed.

The study of the distribution of power in this way can be more objective and more fruitful than in the usual survey methods. Groups of different scopes, sizes and cultures can be compared within different structural situations which lead to the development of informal organisation. Comparison can then be made between the various symbolic strategies which have been adopted by various groups in solving their basic problems in political organisation, taking each one of these problems as a basis for comparison at a time. The organisational potentialities of different symbolic forms can thus be analysed. In this way, different symbolic forms are compared within similar structural situations and similar symbolic forms within different structural situations.

In tackling such issues we are in fact dealing with the basic questions about the nature of politico-symbolic dialectics and their analysis will thus shed substantial light on the major theoretical problems of the political anthropology of modern society.

The crucial politico-symbolic drama

Some of the answers to these problems can be found in the search for and analysis of key dramatic performances that are found in all societies. Social behaviour generally manifests itself phenomenologically in endless series of such performances which thus pervade the whole fabric of social life. These performances have been called 'social dramas' by Turner (1957) and 'sociodrama' by Duncan (1968). Both scholars have made significant contributions to the analysis of the structure and process of these symbolic events. Some of these dramas are more crucial than others for the development, maintenance and functioning of the organisation of a group. It is in these dramas that the political and the symbolic orders interpenetrate and affect one another. Each drama tries to effect a transformation in the psyches of the participants, conditioning their attitudes and sentiments, repetitively renewing beliefs, values and norms and thereby creating and recreating the basic categorical imperatives on which the group depends for its existence. At the same time, some or many of the participants may attempt to manipulate, modify or change the symbols of the drama to articulate minor or major changes in the 'message' of the drama.

Thus, to use examples from my own studies, with which I am more familiar, one of the most crucial politico-symbolic dramas among the Hausa of Ibadan discussed in the last chapter (pp. 92–8) is the divination sessions held daily between laymen and *malams*. In these sessions laymen express their problems and anxieties to the *malams* from whom they expect ritual counsel. In their frequent meetings with one another, these *malams* pool their information and this information passes regularly from the junior to the most senior *malams*. In their divination sessions with the economico-political leaders of the community – the landlords of the trade and the chief – these problems are discussed and some broad lines for solutions emerge. These are passed back down the hierarchy of *malams* and then to laymen in the form of ritual advice on dealing with the afflictions from which these men are currently suffering. The whole revolution in that community's religion during the early 1950s was effected through these divination and consultation sessions between laymen and *malams*. The ritual masters who had received their ritual instructions from the leaders of the Tijaniyya order, initiated in their turn the junior *malams* who then in their turn advised laymen to adopt the order whose *baraka* would solve their basic problems. After that formative period of structural change, the divination session between *malams* and laymen, now modified and institutionalised in the form of a ritual bond between ritual master and initiate, continued to keep alive and maintain the ideology and symbols of the order which now articulated the political organisation of the community.

In the Arab villages discussed above (pp. 114–17) the crucial politico-symbolic drama was that of arranging a marriage. Here the main articulating principle of social organisation is female symbolism, with hardly any exploitation of ritual symbols. The political order in the village is maintained and kept alive through the maintenance of repetitive patterns of the exchange of women within and between the lineages. Although the lineage is organised under the myth of patrilineal descent, men are in fact held together through the sharing of rights and obligations in relation to the daughters and sisters of one another. A political change always becomes involved in a change in the pattern of marriage. The arrangement of every marriage involves political manoeuvring on lineage and on village levels. For this reason, it is in the process of arranging a marriage that the political order and the symbolic order act on one another. Change, both repetitive and structural, is effected through change in the pattern of marriage and the arrangement of every marriage is therefore a politico-symbolic drama of the first order. This is why in my study of one of these villages I found it necessary to present an extended and detailed case of a marriage which became involved in a serious political cleavage in the village and in the general Arab-Jewish cleavage in the whole region (Cohen 1965).

A third example is that of the Friday mid-day prayer in centralised Islamic polities. In Islam, the five daily prayers can be performed individually and in private, but the Friday mid-day prayer must be performed publicly and collectively in a central mosque known as the Friday Mosque. All the mature males of the community must perform the prayer together under the ritual leadership of the chief Imam and the ruler and leaders of the community. A division of the Friday ritual congregation is believed to be fraught with mystical dangers which can bring about the annihilation of the whole community. In the history of many Islamic communities the Friday prayer has been an issue for serious factional disputes, sometimes involving a great deal of violence. The prayer has many political potentialities. It occasions the concentration in one place of all the men of the local community. The presence of the ruler or leader of the community and the symbolic reference to him in the sermon makes every Friday prayer into a demonstration of allegiance to the existing political order. This is why the prayer has always been an ideal strategic occasion in Muslim countries for staging rebellion, as, in the presence of all the men of the community in one gathering, it is possible to assassinate the ruler and to present the congregating men of the community with the fact: the King is dead, long live the King. A serious political cleavage often expresses itself in the establishment of rival Friday mosques and in many situations a struggle for power in a community takes the form of a struggle to control the Friday mosque, often seizing on trivial theological points. (For a more detailed discussion see Cohen 1969b:129–40; 153–60.)

The essence of the drama is the struggle to achieve communion between disparate individuals or potential enemies and to give a tangible expression to this communion. In the course of the drama the struggle is internalised within the psyches of the participants. Here it becomes a struggle for the achievement of selfhood in terms of the symbolism of communion. The individual creates and recreates his oneness through partaking in the symbolism that articulates the corporate organisation of the group of which he is a member.

The relevance of 'mumbo-jumbology'

As indicated earlier, some significant beginnings in the systematic analysis of politico-symbolic dialectics on these lines have already been made by social anthropologists studying simple societies. The most strange and grotesque of customs, like those of witchcraft and sorcery, of the ceremonial exchange of insults in what are known as joking relationships, addresses to the dead and of cults of various sorts, were shown to be systematically interconnected with struggles over power and privilege between individuals and groups of various compositions.

But the strange and the grotesque in behaviour are not the exclusive monopoly of primitive society. 'Mumbo-jumbo' patterns of behaviour are firmly built into the fabric of our social life. The rituals and ceremonies regularly performed by the many millions of rational men – among them doctors, lawyers, and university professors – who are affiliated within the Freemasonic order on both sides of the Atlantic are not inferior in their oddity and eccentricity to the rituals and ceremonies of the most 'primitive' of tribes. The colossal drama staged annually in Red Square in Moscow on May

Day, at staggering costs in manpower and resources, is indeed far more exotic than the annual Earth Cult gathering of the Tallensi or the coronation of the king of the Shilluks. There is no evidence whatever that with the advance of science and enlightenment, or with the coming of the socialist revolution, 'mumbo-jumbo' activities become outdated. The students and lecturers of sociology, political science, economics and other disciplines who staged a powerful demonstration in front of the American embassy in Grosvenor Square in London in 1968 protesting against the war in Vietnam, were 'debunkers' who used their training and intellect to 'expose', 'unmask' the non-rationality of 'establishment mythologies'. But in organising their ranks, they chanted in deafening beat: 'Ho! Ho! Ho Chi Minh . . . Ho! Ho! Ho Chi Minh . . .'. Their behaviour would seem to a Zulu as eccentric as the Zulu war dance would seem to them. They were debunking gods but did so under the banners of new gods.

The ubiquity and necessity of symbolic action and formations in all social systems has been ignored or misunderstood by orthodox Marxists and by some other 'revolutionary' scholars. One of the major functions of symbols is to give tangible relatively enduring objectification to relations that are perennially in the process of 'becoming'. Change is endemic even in the relatively stable socio-cultural systems. The stability of the system is in effect maintained by repetitive symbolic activities which continuously create and recreate the system. The ceremonials of authority have to be periodically staged in order to reassert its existence and its efficacy in the face of the subversive processes of change and anarchy. Symbols achieve this measure of continuity-in-change by their ambiguity and multiplicity of meanings. A ceremonial may be repeated over and over again in the same form though its symbols may be charged with different meanings to accommodate new developments. There is thus a continuous process of action and counteraction between the symbolic order and the power order even when there is no significant structural change.

In his earlier work, Marx clearly saw this process as being *dialectical*, not mechanical. He recognised the fact that the symbolic order, which he labelled as 'superstructure', was not completely determined by the power order, which he labelled as 'infrastructure', but that it had an autonomy of its own. However, as he and many of his followers became increasingly preoccupied with revolution and radical change, they ignored or lost sight of this dialectic. Their formulations became mechanistic and deterministic, explaining away the symbolic in terms of the politico-economic. They thus failed to develop a truly dialectical political anthropology. It is only in recent years that some Marxian sociologists have been trying to make up for this weakness. Thus in a recent paper, Althusser (1971) has recognised the 'recreating' process of ideology, showing how ideology repetitively 'reproduces the conditions of production'.

Yet, some 'progressive' sociologists continue to ignore these theoretical issues and label social anthropologists as 'conservative' in their approach because of their preoccupation with the study of stable systems of relationships. It is crucial for the development of the study of politico-symbolic dialectics to analyse the 'conservative' aspect of symbolism, to see how symbols produce a measure of continuity of social arrangements in 'revolutionary' as well as in 'reactionary' systems. No revolution can be staged or can survive without the manipulation of the symbols of permanence, for without that it cannot relate itself to the people or institutionalise its 'order', and would certainly end up in chaos. A degree of permanence and continuity is an essential condition for any kind of regular social life (Fürer Haimendorf 1967:208–10).

The study of the processes of the conservatism of order need not itself be conservative. The identification and analysis of the symbols of 'student power' is not more progressive or more scientific than the study of the symbols of reactionary movements. The results of such enquiries can benefit the agents of progress as much as the agents of reaction. The study of the processes of continuity does not imply subscription to a creed of continuity. Among the most radical anthropologists of the left are men and women who have built up their academic status on the analysis of some of the most 'traditional', 'conservative', 'stable' societies.

In modern industrial society, no less than in simple society, symbolic patterns of behaviour are as live and as significant as any of the manifestations of order and rationality. We are not always aware of the ubiquity of these patterns because we are immersed in them, because they are part and parcel of our social life and of our very selfhoods. This is why we may learn a great deal about them, or at least identify their existence, when a Nuer or a Tonga anthropologist will one day carry out field work in our midst.

People engage in ritual and ceremony to derive comfort, perform

CONCLUSION

a social obligation, achieve recreation, discover their identity, pass the time, be with others, and for an endless variety of other private personal purposes. But quite apart from these purposes, these patterns of behaviour affect and are affected by relations of power between individuals and groups. A great deal of this involvement of symbolic behaviour in power relations is unintended by the actors. But the two orders, the symbolic and the political, are, nevertheless, interdependent and to some extent 'causally' related. Everywhere political man is also a symbolist man and the analysis of relations between these two dimensions of man's activities holds the key to many of the basic problems in sociology, political science, social psychology, philosophy.

Social anthropology, or 'mumbo-jumbology' as the cynics may like to call it, can make a unique contribution to the behavioural sciences generally by the application of its concepts, theories and techniques to the study of politico-symbolic interdependence in modern complex society. But to do so it will have in its turn to be more rigorously specialised and more systematic than it has been so far. The social anthropologist studying a primitive society had the whole field for himself, covering almost every feature, including ecology, technology, demography, history, law, economics as well as politics. Those features had not been explored by the respective specialists. But as he comes to study large-scale complex society he has to realise that many of these features have been competently and systematically studied by specialists (economists, sociologists, political scientists, psychologists, historians) who, by virtue of their experience and the vast human and material resources at their disposal, can do their job far better than he can. He may of course decide to concentrate on the study of one of these features – economics, law, history – but because of the high standards of specialisation that have become established in these pursuits, he will have neither the time nor the training required to cover other institutional fields. Some anthropologists have indeed done this and have thereby become identified with one or another of the specialised disciplines. But the systematic study of 'custom', of 'the bizarre and the exotic', in modern complex society is still largely unclaimed, even though some of the well established behavioural sciences, like sociology and political science, have sporadically ventured into this field. Now, perhaps more than ever before, is the time to develop a discipline which analyses the interconnections between symbolic action – patterns of 'mumbo-jumbo' behaviour – and power relationships in modern society.

The concepts, theories, methods and general experience of political anthropology can be mobilised to meet this challenge. Its cumulative formulations that have been developed in the study of simple societies can substantially deepen our understanding of the socio-cultural structure of complex society. Political anthropologists are themselves being forced by a variety of circumstances to deal with this problem. But they need to be more analytical and more consciously dialectical in their general approach than they have been so far.

Three major dialectical issues can be subjected to sustained enquiry: symbols and power relations, symbols and selfhood, symbols and change. These are highly interrelated problems. The symbolic order and the power order are involved in the creation and recreation of selfhood and also in the dynamics of continuity and change. The same symbolic formation is intrinsically implicit in all three issues.

This is why a dialectical political anthropology will have to focus on the structure of the drama in relation to power, selfhood and change. Symbolic patterns of activity will have to be analysed in terms of forms, functions and techniques, in their involvement in the distribution and maintenance of power and the struggle for it. They will also have to be analysed in relation to the continuing dialectic of selfhood. Inevitably this will lead to the systematic exploration of artistic creativity which is manifested in the manipulation of existing symbols and the creation of new symbols. The enquiry will have to move to the processes by which individual symbolic innovations are adopted by a group and are thereby transformed into objective collective representations.

The investigation of such issues will shed substantial light on the general processes of symbolisation and of institutionalisation which, as Parsons and Blau point out, are the main concern of sociological enquiry.

Bibliography

ALMOND, G. A., and POWELL, G. B., JR (1966), *Comparative Politics: A Developmental Approach*, Boston: Little, Brown and Company.

ALTHUSSER, L. (1971), 'Ideology and ideological state apparatuses. Notes towards an investigation', from L. Althusser, *Lenin and Philosophy and Other Essays*, New Left Books, 123–73. Reproduced in B. R. Cosin (ed.) (1972), *Education: Structure and Society*, Harmondsworth: Penguin, 242–80.

ARGYLE, MICHAEL (1967), *The Psychology of Interpersonal Behaviour*, Harmondsworth: Penguin.

BAILEY, F. G. (1960), *Tribe, Caste and Nation*, Manchester University Press.

BAILEY, F. G. (1963), *Politics and Social Change*, Berkeley: University of California Press.

BAILEY, F. G. (1969), *Stratagems and Spoils*, Oxford: Blackwell.

BANTON, M. (1957), *West African City*, London: Oxford University Press.

BARNES, J. A. (1968), 'Networks and political process', in M. Swartz (ed.), *Local Level Politics*, Chicago: Aldine.

BARTH, F. (1966), *Models of Social Organisation*, Occasional Paper, London: Royal Anthropological Institute.

BARTH, F. (1967), 'On the study of social change', *American Anthropologist*, 69, 661–9.

BEATTIE, J. H. M. (1959), 'Understanding and explanation in social anthropology', *British Journal of Sociology*, 10, 45–60.

BEATTIE, J. H. M. (1968), 'Aspects of Nyoro symbolism', *Africa*, 38, 413–42.

BECKER, H., *see* WIESE, VON, and BECKER.

BEIDELMAN, T. O. (1968a), 'Some Nuer notions of nakedness, nudity and sexuality', *Africa*, 38, 113–32.

BEIDELMAN, T. O. (1968b), 'Review of V. Turner, *The Forest of Symbols*', *Africa*, 38, 483–4.

BEIDELMAN, T. O. (1969), 'Review of V. Turner, *The Drums of Affliction*', *Africa*, 39, 91–3.

BENTLEY, A. F. (1949), *The Process of Government*, San Antonio: Principia Press of Trinity.

BERGER, PETER L. (1969), *A Rumour of Angels: Modern Society and the Rediscovery of the Supernatural*, London: Allen Lane, the Penguin Press.

BERGER, PETER L. with T. LUCKMAN (1967), *The Social Construction of Reality*, London: Allen Lane, The Penguin Press.

BERMANT, CHAIM (1971), *The Cousinhood: The Anglo-Jewish Gentry*, London: Eyre & Spottiswoode.

BLAU, PETER M. (1969), 'Objectives of sociology', in Robert Bierstedt (ed.), *A Design for Sociology: Scope, Objectives and Methods*, Philadelphia: The American Academy of Political and Social Science.

BOHANNAN, L. (1952), 'A genealogical charter', *Africa*, 22, 301–15.

BOISSEVAIN, J. (1968), 'The place of non-groups in the social sciences', *Man* (new series), 3, 542–56.

CAPLAN, L. (1970), *Land and Social Change in East Nepal*, Berkeley: University of California Press.

CASSIRER, ERNST (1946), *The Myth of the State*, New Haven: Yale University Press.

CASTLES, F. G. (1967), *Pressure Groups and Political Culture*, London: Routledge & Kegan Paul.

CHAPMAN, R. A. (1969), *Decision Making: A case study of the decision to raise the Bank Rate in September 1957*, London: Routledge & Kegan Paul.

COHEN, ABNER (1965) (reprinted 1972), *Arab Border Villages in Israel: A Study of Continuity and Change in Social Organisation*, Manchester University Press.

COHEN, ABNER (1968), 'The politics of mysticism in some local communities in newly independent African states', in M. Swartz (ed.), *Local Level Politics*, Chicago: Aldine.

COHEN, ABNER (1969a), 'Political anthropology: the analysis of the symbolism of power relations', *Man*, 4, 217–35.

COHEN, ABNER (1969b), *Custom and Politics in Urban Africa*, London: Routledge & Kegan Paul; Berkeley: University of California Press.

COHEN, ABNER (1970), 'The politics of marriage in changing middle eastern stratification systems', Plotnicov and Tuden (eds.), *Essays in Comparative Social Stratification*, London: Collier-Macmillan.

COHEN, ABNER (1971), 'The politics of ritual secrecy', *Man* (new series), 6, 427–48.

COHEN, ABNER (1972), 'Scale and political alliance through the exchange of women', mimeographed for Wenner-Gren Symposium, No. 55, on *Scale and Social Organisation*, 14 East 71 St, New York, N.Y. 10021.

COHEN, ABNER (1974), 'The lesson of ethnicity', in A. Cohen (ed.), *Urban Ethnicity*, ASA monograph no. 12, London: Tavistock.

COHEN, E. G. (1973), 'Recruitment to the professional class', unpublished Ph.D. thesis, University of Surrey.

COHEN, P. S. (1968), *Modern Social Theory*, London: Heinemann Educational.

COLSON, E. (1962), *The Plateau Tonga of Northern Rhodesia: Social and Religious Studies*, Manchester University Press.

CUNNISON, I. G. (1959), *The Luapula Peoples of Northern Rhodesia: Custom and History in Tribal Politics*, Manchester University Press.

DAHRENDORF, R. (1968), 'On the origin of inequality among men', *Essays in the Theory of Society*, Stanford University Press, 151–78.

DESHON, S. (1963), 'Compadrazgo on a Henequen Hacienda in Yucatan: A structural revaluation', *American Anthropologist*, 65, 574–83.

DEUTSCH, K. W. (1966), *The Nerves of Government*, New York: The Free Press; London: Collier-Macmillan.

DEVONS, E. *see* GLUCKMAN and DEVONS.

DEWAR, JAMES (1966), *The Unlocked Secret: Freemasonry Examined*, London: William Kimber.

DOUGLAS, M. (1966), *Purity and Danger*, London: Routledge & Kegan Paul.

DOUGLAS, M. (1968), 'The social control of cognition: some factors in joke perception', *Man* (new series), 3, 361–76.

DUNCAN, J. D. (1962), *Communication and Social Order*, London: Oxford University Press.

DUNCAN, J. D. (1968), *Symbols in Society*, New York: Oxford University Press.

DUNCAN, J. D. (1969), *Symbols and Social Theory*, New York: Oxford University Press.

EASTON, D. (1959), 'Political anthropology', in B. J. Siegel (ed.), *Biennial Review of Anthropology*, London: Oxford University Press.

EASTON, D. (1965), *A Framework for Political Analysis*, Englewood Cliffs: Prentice-Hall.

EASTON, D. (1968), 'Political science', *The International Encyclopedia of the Social Sciences*, New York: Macmillan.

ECKSTEIN, H. (1960), *Pressure Group Politics*, London: Allen & Unwin.

EHRMANN, H. W. (ed.) (1964), *Interest Groups on Four Continents*, Pittsburgh University Press.

ESSIEN-UDOM, E. U. (1966), *Black Nationalism*, Harmondsworth: Penguin.

EVANS-PRITCHARD, E. E. (1937), *Witchcraft, Oracles and Magic Among the Azande of the Anglo-Egyptian Sudan*, Oxford: Clarendon Press.

EVANS-PRITCHARD, E. E. (1940a), *The Nuer*, Oxford: Clarendon Press.

EVANS-PRITCHARD, E. E. (1940b), with M. FORTES (eds), 'Introduction', *African Political Systems*, London: Oxford University Press.

EVANS-PRITCHARD, E. E. (1948), *The Divine Kingship of the Shilluk of the Anglo-Egyptian Sudan*, Cambridge University Press.

EVANS-PRITCHARD, E. E. (1949), *The Sanusi of Cyrenaica*, Oxford: Clarendon Press.

EVANS-PRITCHARD, E. E. (1951a), *Kinship and Marriage among the Nuer*, Oxford: Clarendon Press.

EVANS-PRITCHARD, E. E. (1951b), *Social Anthropology*, London: Cohen & West: Chicago: Free Press.

EVANS-PRITCHARD, E. E. (1956), *Nuer Religion*, Oxford: Clarendon Press.

EVANS-PRITCHARD, E. E. (1961), *Anthropology and History*, Manchester University Press.

EVANS-PRITCHARD, E. E. (1963), *The Comparative Method in Social Anthropology*, L. T. Hobhouse Memorial Trust Lecture No. 33, University of London: Athlone Press.

FERRIS, P. (1960), *The City*, Harmondsworth: Penguin.

FINER, S. (1958), *Anonymous Empire*, London: Pall Mall Press.

FIRTH, R. (1951), *Elements of Social Organisation*, London: Watts.

FORTES, M. (1936), 'Ritual festivals and social cohesion in the hinterland of the Gold Coast', *American Anthropologist*, 38, 590–604.

FORTES, M. (1940), and EVANS-PRITCHARD, E. E. (eds), 'Introduction', *African Political Systems*, London: Oxford University Press.

FORTES, M. (1945), *The Dynamics of Clanship among the Tallensi*, London: Oxford University Press.

FORTES, M. (1949), *The Web of Kinship among the Tallensi*, London: Oxford University Press.

FORTES, M. (1950), 'Kinship and marriage among the Ashanti', A. R. Radcliffe-Brown and Daryll Forde (eds), *African Systems of Kinship and Marriage*, London: Oxford University Press.

FORTES, M. (1953), 'Social anthropology at Cambridge since 1900: an inaugural lecture', Cambridge University Press.

FORTES, M. (1959), 'Descent, filiation and affinity: a rejoinder to Dr. Leach', *Man*, 59, 193–7, 206–12.

FORTES, M. (1967), 'Totem and taboo', *Proceedings of the Royal Anthropological Institute, 1966*, 5–22.

FORTES, M. (1968), 'On installation ceremonies', *Proceedings of the Royal Anthropological Institute, 1967*, 5–20.

FOSTER, SIR JOHN G. (1971), *Enquiry into the Practice and Effects of Scientology*, London: HMSO.

FRANKENBERG, R. J. (1957), *Village on the Border*, London: Cohen & West.

FREEDMAN, M. (1958), *Lineage Organization in Southeastern China*, London: Athlone Press.

FREEDMAN, M. (1966), *Chinese Lineage and Society*, London: Athlone Press.

FÜRER-HAIMENDORF, C. VON (1967), *Morals and Merit*, London: Weidenfeld & Nicolson.

GEERTZ, C. (ed.) (1963), *Old Societies and New States*, New York: Free Press.

GEERTZ, C. (1964), 'Ideology as a cultural system', D. Apter (ed.), *Ideology and Discontent*, New York: Free Press.

GEERTZ, C. (1966), 'Religion as a cultural system', Michael Banton (ed.), *Anthropological Approaches to the Study of Religion*, ASA monograph no. 3, London: Tavistock, 1–46.

GLAZER, N. with MOYNIHAN, D. P. (1965), *Beyond the Melting Pot*, Cambridge, Massachusetts: MIT Press.

GLUCKMAN, MAX (1942), *Analysis of a Social Situation in Modern Zululand*, Manchester University Press.

GLUCKMAN, MAX (1950), 'Kinship and marriage among the Lozi of Northern Rhodesia and the Zulu of Natal', in A. R. Radcliffe-Brown and D. Forde (eds), *African Systems of Kinship and Marriage*, London: Oxford University Press.

GLUCKMAN, MAX (1954), *Rituals of Rebellion in South-East Africa*, Manchester University Press.

GLUCKMAN, MAX (1955), *The Judicial Process among the Barotse of Northern Rhodesia*, Manchester University Press.

GLUCKMAN, MAX (1962), 'Les rites de passage', in M. Gluckman, *et al.*, *Essays on the Ritual of Social Relations*, Manchester University Press.

GLUCKMAN, MAX (1963), *Order and Rebellion in Tribal Africa*, London: Cohen & West.

GLUCKMAN, MAX (1964), with E. DEVONS (eds), Introduction and Conclusion of *Closed Systems and Open Minds: The Limits of Naïvety in Social Anthropology*, Edinburgh: Oliver & Boyd.

GLUCKMAN, MAX (1965a), *Politics, Law and Ritual in Tribal Society*, Oxford: Blackwell.

GLUCKMAN, MAX (1965b), with F. EGGAN, 'Introduction', in M. Banton (ed.), *The Relevance of Models for Social Anthropology*, ASA monograph no. 1, London: Tavistock.

BIBLIOGRAPHY

GLUCKMAN, MAX (1968), 'Psychological, sociological and anthropological explanations of witchcraft and gossip: a clarification', *Man* (new series), 3, 20–34.

GLUCKMAN, MAX. (Forthcoming), *Sport and Conflict.*

GOFFMAN, E. (1969), *The Presentation of Self in Everyday Life*, London: Allen Lane, the Penguin Press. (First published in 1959, Anchor Books, USA.)

GOODLAD, J. S. R. (1971), *A Sociology of Popular Drama*, London: Heinemann.

GORDON, ALBERT I. (1964), *Intermarriage: Interfaith, Interracial, Interethnic*, Boston: Beacon Press.

GUDEMAN, STEPHEN (1972), 'The Compadrazgo as a reflection of the natural and spiritual person', *Proceedings of the Royal Anthropological Institute for 1971.*

HANNERZ, ULF (1974), 'Ethnicity and opportunity in urban America', in Abner Cohen (ed.), *Urban Ethnicity*, ASA monograph no. 12, London: Tavistock.

HERBERG, W. (1960), *Protestant, Catholic and Jew*, New York: Anchor Books.

HERNTON, C. C. (1969), *Sex and Racism*, London: Paladin.

HILL, P. (1963), *Migrant Cocoa-Farmers of Southern Ghana*, Cambridge University Press.

HOLTZMAN, ABRAHAM (1966), *Interest Groups and Lobbying*, New York: The Macmillan Company. London: Collier-Macmillan.

HOMANS, G. C. (1951), *The Human Group*, London: Routledge & Kegan Paul.

HUNT, N. C. (1956), 'Pressure groups in the USA', *Occidente, 12.*

JAHODA, GUSTAV (1969), *The Psychology of Superstition*, London: Penguin Books.

KEATLEY, PATRICK (1963), *The Politics of Partnership: The Federation of Rhodesia and Nyasaland*, Harmondsworth: Penguin.

KELLER, S. (1968), *Beyond the Ruling Class: Strategic Elites in Modern Society*, New York: Random House. (First published in 1963.)

KILSON, MARTIN (1967), *Political Change in a West African State*, Cambridge, Mass.: Harvard University Press.

KUPER, H. (1947), *An African Aristocracy: Rank among the Swazi*, London: Oxford University Press.

LANGER, S. (1964), *Philosophical Sketches*, New York: New American Library of World Literature.

LEACH, E. R. (1954), *Political Systems of Highland Burma*, London: Bell.

LEACH, E. R. (1958), 'Magical Hair', *Journal of the Royal Anthropological Institute*, 88, 147–64.

LEACH, E. R. (1961), *Rethinking Anthropology*, London: Athlone Press.

LEACH, E. R. (1967), 'Introduction', in E. R. Leach (ed.), *The Structural Study of Myth and Totemism*, ASA monograph no. 6, London: Tavistock.

LENSKI, G. (1963), *The Religious Factor: A Sociological Enquiry*, New York: Doubleday.

LÉVI-STRAUSS, C. (1968), *Structural Anthropology*, London: Allen Lane, the Penguin Press. (First published in English in 1963.)

LEWIS, I. M. (1971), *Ecstatic Religion*, Harmondsworth: Penguin.

LIENHARDT, R. G. (1964), *Social Anthropology*, London: Oxford University Press.

LITTLE, K. (1965), 'The political functions of the Poro, part 1', *Africa*, 35, 349–65.

LITTLE, K. (1966), 'The political functions of the Poro, part 2', *Africa*, 36, 62–72.

LITTLE, K. (1967), *The Mende of Sierra Leone*, London: Routledge & Kegan Paul.

LLOYD, P. (1955), 'The development of political parties in Western Nigeria', *American Political Science Review*, 49, 693–707.

LLOYD, P. (1965), 'The political structure of African kingdoms: an exploratory model', M. Banton (ed.), *Political Systems and the Distribution of Power*, ASA monograph no. 2, London: Tavistock.

LUCKMAN, T. *see* BERGER and LUCKMAN.

LUPTON, T., and WILSON, S. (1959), 'Background and connections of top decision-makers', *Manchester School*, 30–51.

MACIVER, R. M. (1947), *The Web of Government*, New York: Macmillan.

MACKENZIE, W. J. M. (1967), *Politics and Social Science*, Harmondsworth: Penguin.

MACRIDIS, R. C. (1955), *The Study of Comparative Government*, New York: Random House.

MANNHEIM, K. (1936), *Ideology and Utopia*, London: Routledge & Kegan Paul.

MAQUET, J. J. (1961), *The Premise of Inequality in Ruanda*, London: Oxford University Press.

MARCUSE, HERBERT (1964), *One-Dimensional Man: The Ideology of Industrial Society*, London: Routledge & Kegan Paul.

MARTIN, D. (1965), 'Towards eliminating the concept of secularisation', in Julius Gould (ed.), *Penguin Survey of the Social Sciences*, Harmondsworth: Penguin.

MAYER, A. C. (1962), 'System and network: an approach to the study of political processes in Dewas', in T. Madan and G. Sarana (eds), *Indian Anthropology*, Bombay: Asia Publishing House.

MAYER, A. C. (1966), 'The significance of quasi-groups in the study of complex societies', in M. Banton (ed.), *The Social Anthropology of Complex Societies*, ASA monograph no. 4, London: Tavistock.

MEAD, G. H. (1934), *Mind, Self and Society*, Chicago University Press.

MIDDLETON, J. (1960), *Lugbara Religion*, London: Oxford University Press.

MINTZ, S. W., and WOLF, E. (1950), 'An analysis of ritual coparenthood (Compadrazgo)', *South West Journal of Anthropology*, 6, 341–68.

MINTZ, S. W., and WOLF, E. (1956), 'Canemalar: the subculture of a rural sugar plantation proletariat', in J. Steward (ed.), *The People of Puerto Rico*, Urbana: University of Illinois Press.

MITCHELL, J. C. (1956), *The Kalela Dance*, Manchester University Press for the Rhodes-Livingstone Institute.

MITCHELL, J. C. (1966), 'Theoretical orientations in African urban studies', M. Banton (ed.), *The Social Anthropology of Complex Societies*, ASA monograph no. 4, London: Tavistock.

MORRIS, J. F. (1972), 'Three aspects of the person in social life', in Ralph Raddock (ed.), *Six Approaches to the Person*. London and Boston: Routledge & Kegan Paul, 70–92.

MOYNIHAN, D. P., *see* GLAZER and MOYNIHAN.

MURDOCK, G. P. (1972), 'Anthropology's mythology', *Proceedings of the Royal Anthropological Institute for 1971*, 17–24.

NADEL, S. F. (1951), *The Foundations of Social Anthropology*, Chicago: Free Press.

NEEDHAM, R. (1967), 'Right and left in Nyoro symbolic classification', *Africa*, 37, 425–52.

NICHOLAS, R. W. (1965), 'Factions: a comparative analysis', M. Banton (ed.), *Political Systems and the Distribution of Power*, ASA monograph no. 2, London: Tavistock.

OKONJO, C. (1967), 'The Western Ibo', in P. Lloyd, *et al.* (eds), *The City of Ibadan*, Cambridge University Press.

OSBORN, A. (1968), 'Compadrazgo and Patronage: a Colombian case', *Man* (new series), 3, 593–608.

PACKARD, V. (1961), *The Status Seekers*, Harmondsworth: Penguin. (First published in USA in 1959.)

PARKIN, D. (1974), 'Congregational and interpersonal ideologies in political ethnicity', in A. Cohen (ed.) *Urban Ethnicity*, ASA monograph, no. 12, London: Tavistock.

PARRY, G. (1969), *Political Elites*, London: Allen & Unwin.

PARSONS, TALCOTT (1951), *The Social System*, Chicago: Free Press.

PETERS, E. L. (1960), 'The proliferation of segments in the lineage of the Bedouin of Cyrenaica', *Journal of the Royal Anthropological Institute*, 90, 29–53.

PETERS, E. L. (1963), 'Aspects of rank and status among Muslims in a Lebanese village', in J. Pitt-Rivers (ed.), *Mediterranean Countrymen*, Paris: Mouton.

PETERS, E. L. (1967), 'Some structural aspects of the feud among the camel-herding Bedouin of Cyrenaica', *Africa*, 37, 261–82.

PITT-RIVERS, J. A. (1958), 'Ritual kinship in Spain', *Transactions of the N.Y. Academy of Sciences*, 20, 424–31.

POWELL, G. B., *see* ALMOND and POWELL.

RADCLIFFE-BROWN, A. R. (1952), *Structure and Function in Primitive Society*, London: Cohen & West.

RIESMAN, D., GLAZER, N. and DENNY, R. (1950), *The Lonely Crowd*, New Haven: Yale University Press.

ROBINSON, J. (1969), *The Cultural Revolution in China*, Harmondsworth: Penguin.

SAMPSON, A. (1962), *Anatomy of Britain*, New York and Evanston: Harper & Row.

SCHAPERA, I. (1938), 'Contact between European and native in South Africa: Bechuanaland', in L. P. Mair (ed.), *Methods of Study of Culture Contact in Africa*, London: Oxford University Press.

SIMMEL, GEORG (1950), *The Sociology of Georg Simmel*, trans., and with an Introduction by Kurt H. Wolff, Chicago: Free Press.

SMITH, M. G. (1956), 'On segmentary lineage systems', *Journal of the Royal Anthropological Institute*, 86, 39–80.

SMITH, M. G. (1960), *Government in Zazzau*, London: Oxford University Press.

SRINIVAS, M. N. (1952), *Religion and Society among the Coorgs of South India*, Oxford: Clarendon Press.

SSRC (SOCIAL SCIENCE RESEARCH COUNCIL) (1968), *Research in Political Science*, London.

TURNER, V. W. (1957), *Schism and Continuity in an African Society*, Manchester University Press.

TURNER, V. W. (1964), 'Symbols in Ndembu ritual', in M. Gluckman (ed.), *Closed Systems and Open Minds*, Edinburgh: Oliver & Boyd.

TURNER, V. W. (1968), *The Drums of Affliction*, Oxford: Clarendon Press.

TURNER, V. W. (1969), *The Ritual Process: Structure and Anti-Structure*, Chicago: Aldine.

WATSON, W. (1958), *Tribal Cohesion in a Money Economy*, Manchester University Press.

WIESE, L. VON, and BECKER, H. (1952), 'Institutionalization', in A. McClung Lee (ed.), *Readings in Sociology*, New York: Barnes & Noble, 334–40. (First published in 1932.)

WILLIS, R. (1967), 'The head and the loins: Lévi-Strauss and beyond', *Man* (new series), 2, 519–34.

BIBLIOGRAPHY

WILLMOTT, P., and YOUNG, M. (1957), *Family and Kinship in East London*, London: Routledge & Kegan Paul.

WILSON, B. (1969), *Religion in Secular Society*, Harmondsworth: Penguin. (First published in 1966 by C. A. Watts.)

WILSON, S., *see* LUPTON and WILSON.

WISEMAN, H. V. (1967), 'Introduction: government, politics and political science', in H. V. Wiseman (ed.), *Political Science*, London: Routledge & Kegan Paul.

WOLF, E., *see* MINTZ and WOLF.

YOUNG, M., *see* WILLMOTT and YOUNG.

YOUNG, O. R. (1968), *Systems of Political Science*, Englewood Cliffs: Prentice-Hall.

Author index

AUTHOR INDEX

Foster, J.G., 2
Frankenberg, R.J., 29
Freedman, M., 114
Fürer-Haimendorf, C.von, 136

Geertz, C., 5, 91
Glazer, N., 97, 105
Gluckman, M., 4, 18, 20, 21, 25, 29, 31, 32, 33, 37, 46, 47, 49, 56, 57, 97
Goffman, E., 3, 34, 53
Goodlad, J.S.R., 29
Gordon, A.I., 72
Gudeman, S., 25

Hannerz, Ulf, 97
Herberg, W., 105
Hernton, C.C., 72
Hill, P., 70
Holtzman, A., 123
Homans, G.C., 21, 53
Hunt, N.C., 123

Jahoda, G., 2

Keatley, P., 72
Keller, S., 129
Kilson, M., 109
Kuper, H., 25, 46

Langer, S., 5
Leach, E.R., x, 4, 21, 25, 30, 33, 34, 43, 47
Lenski, G., 105
Lévi-Strauss, C., 5, 43, 45, 71
Lewis, I.M., 47
Lienhardt, R.G., 47
Little K., 109
Lloyd, P., 126
Luckman, T., 37, 41, 59
Lupton, T., 99

MacIver, R.M., x
Mackenzie, W.J.M., 127, 128
Macridis, R.C., 76
Mannheim, K., 8
Maquet, J.J., 130
Marcuse, H., 64, 88
Martin, D., 25
Marx, K., 5, 22, 32, 110, 120, 122, 129, 135
Mayer, A.C., 40, 126

Mead, G.H., 41
Middleton, J., 47, 114
Mintz, S.W., 25
Mitchell, J.C., 29, 124
Morris, J.F., 55
Moynihan, D.P., 97, 105
Murdock, G.P., 9

Nadel, S.F., 34
Needham, R., 44
Nicholas, R.W., 40

Okonjo, C., 92
Osborn, A., 25

Packard, V., 71, 122
Parkin, D., 91
Parry, G., 99
Parsons, T., 5, 138
Peters, E.L., 24, 46, 47, 69, 70
Pitt-Rivers, J.A., 25
Powell, G.B., 49

Radcliffe-Brown, A.R., 18, 21, 32, 41, 54
Riesman, D., 88
Robinson, J., 39

Sampson, A., 99, 110
Schapera, I., 126
Simmel, G., 110, 129
Smith, M.G., 20, 32, 89
Srinivas, M.N., 121
SSRC (Social Science Research Council), 127

Turner, V.W., 4, 21, 24, 45, 50, 55, 56, 57, 132

Watson, W., 25
Weber, M., xi, 5, 40, 120
Wiese, L.von, 53
Willis, R., 44
Wilmott, P., 27
Wilson, B., 2, 61
Wilson, S., 99
Wolf, E., 25,

Young, M., 27,
Young, O.R., 7

Subject index

Accent, 99
Action sets, 40
Action theorists, 40–3
Affinity, 16, 34, 73, 98, 99, 111; *see also*
  Alliance, Cousinhood, Marriage
African societies, 67, 92
African studies, 51, 102, 126
Alliance, 16, 71, 73, 114; *see also* Affinity,
  Cousinhood, Marriage
America, *see* USA
American tourists, 70–1
Americo-Liberians, 101
Analysis, sociological and anthropological,
  13, 39–40, 45–7
Ancestors, 26; cult of 69, 114–15; *see also*
  Dead, cult of
Anomie, 60
Anthropology, political and social, 8–13,
  19, 33, 45, 124
Arab(s), 17, 31, 46; lineages, 76, 114–15;
  peasants, 73; villages, 70, 114–18, 133;
  world, 72
Art, 6, 30,
Artists, 30, 63, 82
Ashanti, 78
Association(s), 14, 53, 54, 66, 68, 119;

tribal, 92, 93, 125; *see also* Organisation
Authority, 36, 46, 60, 77–80, 98, 103, 109,
  118, 123; ceremonials of, 135; composite
  nature of, 122; ritual, 104; symbols of,
  31, 32
Azande, 62

Badges, 74
Banqueting, 109
Baraka, 104
Bedouin of Cyrenaica, 24, 70
Begging industry, 97
Belief(s), 81, 82–4
Biographies, 66
Black Muslims, 74, 105
Boundaries, *see* Distinctiveness, group
British society, 27
Brotherhood, 43, 104; *see also* Fraternities,
  Freemasonry
Bunyoro, 45
Bureaucracy, 12, 49, 66
Burial, 62; *see also* Death

Carving, 30
Case-studies, 14–17, 90–117

Poro, 109
Potlatching, 74
Power, ix, xi, 7, 10, 16, 22, 31, 33, 43, 65, 77, 94, 122
Power relations, 18–34 *passim*, 45; *see also* Relationships
Prayer, 53, 133–4
Primary relationships, 73–4, 79, 85, 90, 98, 99, 100
Privacy, 15, 129
Psychic processes, 4, 21, 134
Psychoanalysis, 55
Psychology, 3–4, 56
Public schools, 99

Quantification, 52, 53

Race, 72
Radical anthropologists, 136
Recreation, 56, 137
Regalia, 74
Relationships, 5, 23, 24, 25, 30, 75; multiplex, 49; power, ix, 17; primary, 73; ritualised, 25
Relativism, cultural, 10
Religion, 2, 7, 15, 22, 26–7, 49, 61–2, 63, 119, 120
Religious cleavages, 72
Retribalisation, *see* Ethnicity, Tribalism
Revolutions, 38; cultural, 39
Rhetoric, 30
Rhodesia, 72, 77, 118
Right(s), 77
Rites of passage, 62
Ritual, 3, 4, 10, 15, 23, 24, 43, 64, 68, 72–3, 137; groups, 91, 102–10; mechanisms, 83; of rebellion, 57; secret, 106–10; symbolism, 50
Ritualisation, 49–50
Role(s), 31, 50, 54, 55, 60, 78
Rothschild family, 111
Ruanda, 101, 130
Rules, 30, 32
Russia, 38

Sabo, 92–8; *see also* Hausa
Samuel family, 111
Sanusi of Cyrenaica, 19–20

Sassoon family, 111
Scientology, 2
Seclusion of women, 117
Secrecy, 129
Secret ritual, 15, 79; groups, 106–10 *passim*
Secret societies, 106–10 *passim*
Sects, 73
Secularisation, 26, 49, 105
Selfhood, x, 4, 32, 36, 41, 54–60, 63, 81, 85, 89, 134, 136, 138
Sentiments, 16, 132
Sex, 72
Shilluk, 46
Sickness, 60
Sierra Leone, 42, 43, 61, 67, 107–10, 112–18 *passim*, 124
Sign, 24
Slogans, 30
Social anthropology, 9–13, 49, 52, 137; challenge to, 29; *see also* Anthropology
Social drama 132; *see also* Drama
Social field, 126
Social order, 32, 38
Social personality, 41, 54
Social psychology, 53, 137
Social structure, 50
Social surplus, 53
Socialisation, 16, 41, 82–4, 98, 117, 118
Sociology, 6–8, 9, 10, 12, 13, 49, 52, 68, 120–1, 123, 137, 138
Sororities, 117
South Africa, 72, 77, 118
Spirit possession, 47
Sports, 3
Stability, social, 18, 31, 57
State, the, 7, 10, 92, 126–9
Statistics, 52–3
Status, 123, 124
Stratification, social, 119–38 *passim*
Structural functionalism, 48
Structuralists, thought, 43–5
Students' power, 136
Style of life, 15, 16, 26, 42, 68, 74, 75, 88, 91, 99, 101, 123, 124, 129
Sufi orders, 73, 79, 103–6; *see also* Tijaniyya
Superstructure, 38, 135
Swazi, 25, 46